Great Stories from History

Here are fourteen great stories from history
bringing the past dramatically alive.
Excitingly and realistically illustrated by
Fortunino Matania the stories are also
brought 'to life' by documents, coins,
sculptures and maps.

The stories come from many countries: the
strange life of Calamity Jane, a heroine of
the American Wild West; Julius Caesar's
two raids on Britain; the spectacular career
of the 'Scourge of God', Attila the Hun; and
other tales, some familiar, others little
known, all vividly presented.

3bcd

GREAT STORIES FROM HISTORY

Illustrated by Fortunino Matania

COVER BY DAVID WILLIAMS

CAROUSEL EDITOR: ANNE WOOD

CAROUSEL BOOKS
A DIVISION OF TRANSWORLD PUBLISHERS LTD
A NATIONAL GENERAL COMPANY

GREAT STORIES FROM HISTORY
A CAROUSEL BOOK 0 552 54023 4

Originally published in Great Britain by Sidgwick
and Jackson Ltd.

PRINTING HISTORY
Sidgwick and Jackson edition published 1970
Carousel edition published 1972

Carousel Books are published by
Transworld Publishers Ltd., Cavendish House,
57-59 Uxbridge Road, Ealing, London W.5.

Made and printed in Great Britain by
C. Nicholls & Company Ltd.

Fortunino Matania at work in his London studio. Every
drawing was the product of deep research. All his life he
was fascinated by finding out what the past really looked
like. He spent much of his time poring
over old documents and illustrations and examining objects
in museums. His rambling house in London overflowed
with all kinds of historical items – costumes, swords,
period furniture, and death masks. If he was unable
to find something that he wanted to draw, he made it
himself in his basement studio.

CONTENTS

CONTRIBUTORS: Peter Newark; Brenda Ralph
Lewis; John Gibert; Beth
Williams; Edward Horton;
Peter Shellard

EDITORS: Edward Horton; Peter Shellard

DESIGN: Ken Carroll; Bob Burroughs

RESEARCH: Bruce Bernard; Mary Dru; Jane
Drake

PICTURE SOURCES AND CREDITS

The man who challenged the might of Rome-and won

Arminius, a German hero

Thunder and lightning crashed and ripped across the dark German sky. Torrential rain beat down on the miserable ranks of the Roman legionaries as they struggled through the tangled undergrowth of the Teutoburg Forest. Quintilius Varus, the Roman governor, wiped the streaming rain from his face, and must have cursed the foul German weather and the rebellious Germans who had brought him to this strange, eerie forest. When he came upon them he would teach the barbarians a lesson they would never forget. It was September in the year A.D. 9.

As the legions of Rome pressed on slowly and wearily, hostile eyes watched their progress from the darkness of the trees. The forest was filled with German tribesmen who, united for the first time under their Roman-trained war leader Arminius, waited eagerly yet patiently for the signal to spring from ambush and strike down the invaders. It was time to teach the Romans a lesson *they* would never forget.

It was Augustus, Emperor of Rome from 27 B.C. to A.D. 14, who had sent his famous legions marching into Germany in 12 B.C. He wanted to extend the frontier of Roman-occupied Gaul (ancient France) beyond the defensive bastion along the River Rhine to the River Elbe, deep in north Germany. This decision had been made in order to stop the infuriating raids of the wild German tribes over the Rhine and into Gaul. Augustus determined to invade and conquer Germany as Caesar had conquered Gaul.

He assigned the task to his favourite stepson, Drusus, who crossed the Rhine, won several major victories, and occupied large portions of the land. But in his hour of triumph Drusus fell from his horse and received injuries from which he died. His brother Tiberius continued the task of conquering 'the land of the barbarians', and succeeded in taking much of central Germany. Tiberius spent several years in the Rhineland, pacifying and civilizing the new Roman territory.

The Germans came to respect Tiberius because of his military strength and his firm but tolerant ways of dealing with them. Any ideas of rebellion against Roman rule were wrecked because the German tribes constantly quarrelled with each other, instead of uniting against the common enemy. It seemed that, with Tiberius as governor, the tribes would soon be tamed, and that occupied Germany would become absorbed as a peaceful province of the Roman Empire.

One of the methods used by the Romans to pacify the restless tribes was to educate and train the young Teutonic nobles so that they might serve Rome as loyal soldiers and guardians. Arminius, or Hermann, as the Germans call him, the Prince of the Cherusci tribe, was one of them. Born about 12 B.C., he went to Rome and was trained in the arts of war. He proved an outstanding soldier and his promotion was rapid. He distinguished himself in battle and was made a Roman citizen.

Arminius returned to Germany in command of a cohort of 1,000 auxiliaries (foreign troops) in the service of the Emperor Augustus. Now that he was back in his homeland, Arminius decided to take a wife. Thusnelda, daughter of Segestes, another Cheruscan chief, caught his eye, and he set about winning her love. She responded to his attentions but her father – because of an old tribal feud – opposed the marriage. Arminius was determined that he should not be denied, so he kidnapped the willing Thusnelda and carried her away on his horse. This earned him the lifelong enmity of her father.

Arminius might never have made his particular mark in history had it not been for the ruthless, grasping, and incompetent behaviour of Quintilius Varus, who succeeded Tiberius as governor of Germany.

Varus had served as governor of Judea, where he had ruled with great harshness; and he tried to apply the same brutal measures against the fierce tribes of north Germany. He sought to abolish their ancient customs, to impose crippling taxes, and to discipline the unruly barbarians. But where Tiberius had won grudging respect, Varus reaped only bitter hatred.

Rebellion smouldered among the tribes, but this was the only common ground between them. What was sorely needed was a leader with the personality and skill to unite the tribes against the oppression.

For all his Roman ways Arminius was a German patriot at heart. The cruel methods and arrogant rule of Varus filled him with a growing anger. If the tyrant governor were not checked the proud tribes would be reduced to nothing more than slaves; and so Arminius developed a plan to free his people.

The Roman legionaries flounder in the thick mud of the forest, at the mercy of the long lances of the Germans.

In doing so he lived a dangerous double life, never far from discovery and death. In one role he served as an officer under the hated Varus. And in the other he was a secret rebel, meeting tribal chieftains and organizing a cohesive fighting force. It was not an easy task. As a Roman officer he was not at first trusted by the suspicious tribesmen. But he finally convinced them of his sincerity, and the promise of freedom from Roman rule brought many chiefs under his command.

Segestes was not involved in the plot, and when he learned of Arminius's intrigue he went to tell Varus the little he knew. But the complacent governor ignored the warning; he believed that the tribes were far too busy fighting each other to challenge his formidable legions. His men were in fortified positions and he thought the barbarians would never dare attack them.

He was right. But Arminius had already decided that to defeat the Romans he must draw them out of their forts and lure them into the dark forests of Germany. To bring this situation about, Arminius initiated a small rebellion in the summer of A.D. 9. He then persuaded the vainglorious governor to march out and crush the revolt. Varus was seeking military prestige to further his political ambitions in Rome and he swallowed the bait.

Varus set forth with three glittering legions, as well as cavalry and auxiliaries, numbering some 30,000 men, to quell the uprising and punish the tribes. Arminius's cohort marched at the rear. When the expedition reached the gloomy Teutoburg Forest, Arminius and his troops quietly left the marching column unnoticed, and vanished into the trees to join up with the waiting, watching Germans who lay in ambush.

Varus and his men struggled deeper and deeper into the dense forest. A thunderstorm exploded and heavy rain drenched the legions and turned the ground to thick mud. Then Arminius decided the time had come to strike. The blowing of horns signalled the attack. The Germans broke cover and fell upon the weary and thoroughly surprised Romans with terrifying war cries and deadly battle axes.

After the first stunning onslaught which cost them many men, the disciplined legionaries closed into solid iron ranks and Arminius, trained as he was in Roman warfare, wisely withdrew his warriors. He wanted to dictate the way of the battle. Varus, knowing that he must get out of the forest trap and reach the plain where his men could then fight in the traditional style, ordered the columns to resume the march; and, incompetent to the last, he insisted that his troops maintain their parade-like formations, which were so unsuited to the forest and broken ground.

As the Romans stumbled blindly on, the Germans showered them with spears from the safety of the trees. Hacked and harried at every step, the lost legions staggered through the thick underbrush. The running battle raged for three days, and the Romans, unable to shake off the relentless Germans, were eventually reduced to an exhausted and panic-stricken rabble. The vast forest engulfed them like a tomb.

Arminius judged the moment perfectly and as a final assault sent in his cavalry. His terrifying horsemen charged into the enemy, and the once-disciplined legionaries broke ranks and fled, every man for himself. Varus did not run. In utter despair he killed himself by falling upon his sword. His legions were completely destroyed. Thousands surrendered but were massacred on the spot. Only a few managed to escape the murderous revenge of the Germans and leave the forest alive.

When the shattering news of the disaster reached Rome, the Emperor Augustus is said to have been plagued with nightmares, waking up in the night, crying, 'Varus, Varus, give me back my legions!' That their army had been annihilated by barbarians was a bitter enough pill for the Romans to swallow, but even more galling was the knowledge that the enemy had been led by a Roman-trained German.

The Germans celebrated their great victory and fêted their brilliant leader. But Arminius's triumph was short-lived. He had hoped that the tribes would remain united and elect him as their King. But the fickle tribesmen, having defeated their Roman masters, continued to fight among themselves. Segestes intrigued against Arminius and, at the head of a group of other chieftains, he took Arminius and Thusnelda prisoner.

Time passed, and Rome, under its new emperor Tiberius – the same Tiberius who had been governor of Germany – recovered from the shock defeat and demanded revenge. Tiberius sent a large army under Germanicus, his nephew, to renew the attempt to conquer Germany. Arminius escaped from captivity, and, faced with the Roman invasion, once again succeeded in uniting the tribes to combat the common enemy.

After laying waste large areas of the country Germanicus and his legions became bogged down by

Arminius's wife, Thusnelda, with her young son stands aloof from her Roman captors. She had been betrayed to the Romans by her own father, Segestes. Arminius swore to exact revenge on the Roman troops stationed in Germany.

marshland and hindered by forest. He abandoned the campaign and withdrew his troops to fortified positions. The treacherous Segestes threw in his lot with Germanicus, delivered him Thusnelda as a prisoner, and then sought safety himself in Roman Gaul.

When Arminius learned the news about Thusnelda he swore to destroy the legions of Germanicus as he had destroyed the army of Varus. When the Romans sent another expedition into Germany, Arminius engaged them in battle. He came off badly this time, and although Germanicus claimed victory, the latter was forced to retreat to the security of the Rhine forts.

In Rome, Tiberius had become weary of the long and unsuccessful attempt to conquer Germany; the military venture had imposed a severe drain on the manpower and resources of the empire. Tiberius recalled Germanicus and his legions from Germany, saying, 'Let the barbarians destroy each other.'

And so it was. For with the Romans gone, the tribes continued their bloody struggle for power, fighting savagely among themselves. Maroboduus, the powerful King of Bohemia, attacked the tribes of the north who were led by Arminius, but he was defeated. For all Arminius's great talent for leadership, however, he himself was the target of much intrigue, and he died by an assassin's dagger in A.D. 21.

Nevertheless, he had fulfilled his destiny. It was because of him that the Romans never conquered Germany. Tacitus, the Roman historian, later wrote of Arminius: 'He was without doubt Germany's liberator. He dared to challenge Roman power not in its weakened state, as others did, but in the fullness of its strength. He may have lost single battles, but in war he was never defeated.'

Arminius is regarded as Germany's first national hero. And in the middle of the 19th century a colossal bronze statue of him was erected on a hill overlooking the Teutoburg Forest. He stands there today, with his sword raised defiantly towards the sky. Visitors can climb stairs inside the high monument and, at the top, from inside the helmet, they can gaze out over the dark forest where Arminius and his tribesmen destroyed the iron legions of Rome.

King Henry IV of England was at Windsor in January 1400, preparing for a Twelfth Night tournament. He was looking forward to an occasion that promised to be exciting and colourful.

Suddenly, while he was waiting, startling news was brought to him by the Duke of York. Conspirators were about to gather in the village of Colnbrook, near Windsor. They were going to overthrow Henry and

'There are traitors among us'
The plot to kill Henry IV

The plotters scheme to bring about King Henry's death. They might have succeeded had they not been betrayed by one of their number. It was a narrow escape for the King.

replace on the throne his cousin, ex-King Richard II, who had been forced to abdicate from the throne three months earlier. Instead of enjoying the tournament Henry was to find himself fleeing for his life to London.

Henry IV had recently overthrown Richard II, and confined him in a cold, cheerless dungeon in Pontefract Castle, Yorkshire. This conspiracy was to be Henry's first experience of the problems of a usurper. Actually, Henry fitted far better than Richard the image of what a king should be, even though Richard had been king by rightful succession. Richard had been far too effeminate for the nobles' liking, with his love of fine clothes, poetry, and painting. He had also treated the nobles with disdain, refusing them a share in the government of England. Henry had good cause to hate him because, after sending him into exile, Richard had arrogantly seized the lands Henry's father had left him. As an exile, Henry had found himself a natural focus for discontent, and when he returned to England to reclaim his inheritance, he found that many nobles were prepared to support him in a bid for the throne itself. That bid had been successful, and on 30 September 1399, Richard had formally 'abdicated'.

But there were still some nobles who wanted to put Richard back on the throne. Four of them – the Earls of Salisbury, Kent, Gloucester, and Essex – had remained loyal to Richard during the abdication crisis. In the ordinary way they could have expected to pay with their heads for this loyalty; but Henry was generous towards them. Instead they spent less than three weeks in prison and were released in early November 1399, with no conditions attached. A month later the Earl of Kent was even sitting on King Henry's Council.

As he fled to the safety of London Henry must have regretted being so lenient. For it was these very Earls who were conspiring against him.

They hatched the plot at Westminster, and the other conspirators included the Abbot of Westminster, the Earl of Rutland, and Richard Maudelyn, a priest who looked remarkably like the deposed King.

The plan was simple. The Twelfth Night tournament at Windsor, which Henry had already announced, would be a perfect opportunity to introduce armed men into the castle. Once inside, these men could open the gates and let in the main rebel army. Henry would then be disposed of with ease, together with his sons, while Maudelyn would pose as King Richard until the real Richard was rescued from Pontefract Castle. The conspirators agreed to gather at Colnbrook, on 6 January.

However, the plot was doomed from the very beginning. There seems to have been little mutual trust between the conspirators for they had to draw up formal bonds of loyalty to each other. The Earl of Rutland was a particularly untrustworthy man. The first thing he did on receiving a confidential reminder of the Colnbrook rendezvous was to show the letter to his father, the Duke of York. York went straight to Henry.

The King decided it was too dangerous to stay at Windsor. He ordered horses to be saddled and in the late afternoon of 4 January, he and his sons sped out of Windsor Castle and galloped hard for London. By nine that evening, they were safely inside the capital.

Immediately, Henry issued warrants for the arrest of the conspirators, and alerted the sheriffs of five counties to prepare their forces. Lookouts were posted at the ports since it was feared that the French, as fellow countrymen of Richard's young wife, Isabella, would come to the rebels' aid.

Within twenty-four hours of reaching London, Henry had gathered together an army of 16,000 archers. By the following day, 6 January, the numbers had swollen to 20,000.

The conspirators now realized that Henry had slipped through their net, but it was too late for them to turn back. If they did not somehow manage to destroy Henry then he would certainly destroy them. Horsemen were sent out to spread the rumour that Henry had fled for his life, and that Richard had escaped from Pontefract and was heading south with an army.

Meanwhile, the Earl of Kent rode to Sunninghill, near Windsor, where the young ex-Queen Isabella was. When he arrived he tore Henry's badges off the coats of Isabella's attendants, and assured the eleven-year-old girl that she would soon be Queen once more. Kent made arrangements for Isabella to proceed to Cirencester in Gloucestershire, and then left to rejoin his fellow-conspirators.

Together, the conspirators rode to Colnbrook, where they were met by the Earl of Rutland, whose treachery was unknown to them. Rutland brought with him the ominous news that Henry was approaching with very strong forces, and after a hurried conference, the conspirators decided to escape westwards, where they might hope to make a successful stand in Wales and Cheshire, both of which were strongly pro-Richard.

None of them ever got there. Henry caught up with them before long, and the rebels scattered. By nightfall, the leaders had stumbled into Cirencester, where they took possession of a house. The next morning, at dawn, they were woken abruptly by a hail of arrows, stones, and lances.

The people of Cirencester had barred all the exits to the house, and were bombarding them through the doors and windows. Anyone who managed to get outside was attacked by the women, who were waiting in the streets armed with all sorts of weapons, including pans of boiling water.

For five hours the siege continued, until finally, at nine in the morning, the townspeople broke into the house and the rebel leaders surrendered. They were marched in triumph to the Abbey of Austin Canons, in the centre of Cirencester. The people, aware of the importance of their captives, promised to spare their lives until they had had the chance of an audience with King Henry. But in the excited atmosphere, violence lay only a little way below the surface.

The rebel leaders had been in custody only six hours when a fire broke out in the town. Almost at once, the rumour spread that the fire was a ruse to cover the rebels' escape, and soon a mob was battering at the gates of the Abbey yelling for the prisoners to be brought out. Those guarding them tried to resist, but the mob swarmed in, dragged the Earls of Kent and Salisbury into the street, and beheaded them on the spot. Then their heads were thrown into a basket and taken to Henry 'like fish for the market'.

The Earls of Gloucester and Huntingdon managed to escape from Cirencester, but Gloucester had not got far before he was captured and taken to Bristol. On 15 January, his head was chopped off and sent to London. The Earl of Huntingdon managed to reach London, where he took a small boat and tried to escape to France. He got no further, however, than the marshes

The leaders of the plot were dragged from the burning building into the street and beheaded.

on the north shore of the Thames in Essex. For several days he lived the life of a fugitive, and finally took shelter in a friend's house. There, his pursuers caught up with him and took him to Chelmsford in Essex, where a mob nearly seized him.

They were forestalled by King Henry's mother-in-law, the Countess of Hereford. The Countess had suffered much in the days of Richard's reign, and now she planned to revenge herself on Huntingdon, who had tried to restore the King she hated. She had him locked up in her castle.

A few days later, Huntingdon was hauled out of his cell, pushed roughly across a makeshift block and beheaded with terrible brutality by an inexperienced headsman, one of his own followers.

As was the custom, the heads of all four rebel Earls were stuck on poles and displayed at London Bridge, as a grisly warning to anyone who might be tempted to follow their example. Judging by later events, the warning went unheeded, for this was only the first of many revolts Henry had to face.

However, for the moment, the King was triumphant. A *Te Deum* was sung at St. Paul's in London to celebrate his victory, and thanks were offered to the Virgin Mary for 'rescuing the most Christian King from the fangs of the wolves and the jaws of wild beasts, who had prepared above our backs a gallows mixed with gall and hated us with a wicked hate.'

It was all very emotional, but Henry was far too shrewd to believe that this loyalty was universal. The speech he made to a gathering of prelates contained a vision of the disturbed future and a threat of how Henry would deal with it. 'Fine sight it were to see us all assembled thus, if all were true and loyal,' he said.

17th-century painting of Pontefract castle, where Richard was imprisoned.

'But there are traitors among us, and I will gather up the tares and cast them out, and set good plants in my garden, and my garden shall be all within my walls and ditches – unless some of you repent.'

The conspiracy sealed the deposed King's fate. Before the end of January, Richard was dead. Just how he died remains a mystery, though the version most widely believed was that he was starved to death inside the grim, dank walls of Pontefract Castle, where the cold alone would have been enough to kill a man of Richard's frail constitution. Then, a few months later, Henry sent Isabella back to her father in France.

But Henry's problems were not over. In September of the same year there was a revolt in Wales. The rebel leader, Owen Glendower, declared his intention of deposing Henry and giving the crown of England to Edmund Mortimer, Earl of March, who had at least as good a claim to the throne as Henry.

So began the inter-family rivalries which Henry's usurpation loosed on England. In breaking the lawful succession, Henry had weakened the authority of the crown, and made it a plaything for anyone to seize who had as good a claim to it as he did. There were many such claimants, and the end result was to be a long and violent civil war – the Wars of the Roses.

A great artist clashes with a Pope
The wrath of Michelangelo

Michelangelo Buonarroti was an Italian sculptor and painter of great genius who was born in 1475 and died in 1564. His most famous work was the ceiling of the Sistine Chapel of the Vatican Palace in Rome. He alone painted this vast and difficult area with a brilliant series of Biblical scenes. The work took him four arduous years.

The task had been commissioned by Pope Julius II, the autocratic ruler of Rome, and patron of the arts. The Pope was an extremely impatient man and expected a work of art to be finished almost as soon as it was started. He was accustomed to immediate obedience.

Michelangelo, on the other hand, was a painstaking perfectionist who would not be hurried; he was also outspoken and temperamental, subject to sudden and violent outbursts of anger. Little wonder that the relationship between these two men was a stormy one.

Michelangelo began work on the Sistine Chapel in May 1508. He painted the ceiling from a wooden scaffold some sixty feet high; it proved a difficult and exhausting job. Michelangelo would allow no one to see his work in its unfinished state, and none dared enter the Chapel lest they triggered off his explosive temper. He would toil in solitary dedication all day, snatch a few hours' sleep, and then work all night with a candle fixed to a paper hat.

But Pope Julius, being a very impatient man, could not wait until the work was finished to gaze upon it. So one day he crept into the Chapel, in disguise, to see how Michelangelo was progressing. The artist saw him and, not knowing – or caring – who the intruder was, hurled down planks and drove him out.

Even so, Julius would not be denied, and another day he marched openly into the Chapel and climbed the long ladder to the scaffold.

'When will it be ready?' he asked the artist.

'When it is ready,' replied Michelangelo.

This answer infuriated the Pope and he struck Michelangelo with his stick. The two men glared at each other angrily. But when the artist threatened to leave Rome the Pope apologized.

When the ceiling paintings were all but completed the Pope could wait no longer. Again he climbed the ladder in the Chapel and once more asked the weary artist when the job would be finished.

'It will be done,' said Michelangelo, 'when it will be done.'

Again the impatient Pope flew into a rage: 'Do you want to be thrown down from this scaffold?'

By now the artist was too exhausted by his years of hard labour to argue or resist the Pope's demand that the task should be finished forthwith. And so the scaffold was taken down even though the paintings were not fully completed. When the Chapel was open to public view in October 1512, the ceiling frescoes were hailed as the marvel of the day, and Michelangelo as the greatest of Italian artists.

Even after 450 years the ceiling of the Sistine Chapel remains one of the greatest achievments in the history of art. Over the centuries countless thousands have gazed in wonder at the magnificent paintings, the immortal work of one man, driven on by his own destiny and an impatient Pope.

Caesar's Raid

55 B.C.–Julius Caesar invades Britain

A Roman galley draws near the shore of Britain. The might of Rome was about to be launched against a tiny, unknown island.

Towards the late summer of 55 B.C., a hollow-cheeked, thin-lipped man, forty-five years old, surveyed what he called 'Oceanus', the stretch of water which separated him from what he hoped would be his next conquest. Thirty miles or so away there lay an island which, according to hopeful informants, contained a wealth of pearls and many gold mines.

This information was highly exaggerated, if not completely untrue, but in any case, Julius Caesar was less interested in such travellers' tales than in the fact that the islanders of Britain had actively encouraged their Celtic kinsmen, the Gauls, whose country Caesar had recently overrun.

To a large extent Britain was an unknown quantity, and with autumn fast approaching there was no time for the usual patient Roman tactics – sapping the morale of the enemy through propaganda and subversion. There was no time either for obtaining important information about the nature of the country; its size, its harbours, and the methods and means of fighting employed by its inhabitants.

Caesar had tried to extract this knowledge from the Veneti, a tribe living in Brittany, whose barge-like ships regularly plied the Channel to trade with the Britons. That he learned nothing from the Veneti was hardly surprising, considering the fact that their recent defeat by the Romans had been marked by the massacre of their nobility and the sale into slavery of most of their population.

However, while Caesar learned nothing, the Britains learned a good deal, because the Veneti lost no time in telling them of the great Roman's interest in their island And though they regarded Rome as some remote, distant place, the Britons already knew a lot about Caesar and the powerful Roman army. The Roman conquest of Gaul had taken eight years, and during that time the news had filtered through to Britain of the unique discipline of this professional fighting force which was conquering the world with its short Spanish broadswords, javelins, and large square shields.

The Britons heard, too, of Roman battle tactics, such as the use of the *testudo* or 'tortoise': while their adversaries attacked in confused hordes, the Roman soldiers made themselves into an armoured column with overlapping shields, and from beneath its safety stabbed at their attackers.

Knowing all this, the Britons tried to play for time. While they were frantically preparing for defence they sent representatives to Caesar at Boulogne to assure him they had come 'to offer their submission to Rome'.

When these Britons returned across the Channel, they were accompanied by Caesar's ambassador, Commius, King of the Atrebates, one of the Gallic tribes. With Commius went a troop of thirty horsemen, and Caesar's instructions 'to visit as many of the tribes as possible, to persuade them to place themselves under the protection of Rome, and to announce that Caesar himself would shortly be arriving'.

In the meantime Caesar had sent a scout, Volusenus, to Britain to reconnoitre the coast for suitable landing places. Unfortunately, Volusenus was a timid explorer: he was, perhaps, rather frightened by the stories then current in the Roman ranks about the wild Britons and their priest-magicians the Druids. Volusenus kept so far away from the shore that he could give Caesar only a vague outline of what to expect.

However, if Caesar remained relatively ignorant of British geography, he soon witnessed at first hand a sample of the violent unpredictable weather that could rage up and down the Channel at almost any time. At Ambleteuse, a tiny port about seven miles from Boulogne, the ships which were intended to transport Caesar's cavalry to Britain were confined to harbour by strong winds. Caesar needed these ships because the ones at Boulogne were not large enough to carry both the cavalry and the infantry. In the end, an impatient Caesar sent the cavalry to Ambleteuse to join the ships, rather than wait until they could make their way to Boulogne. He then embarked his two legions – the Seventh and the Tenth – comprising 10,000 men, onto the eighty ships at Boulogne. Infantry and cavalry, he decided, would have to meet up on the other side of the Channel.

Caesar sailed at midnight a few days later, and at about nine the next morning the white cliffs of Dover came into sight. As he stood on deck and surveyed the hordes of Britons lining the cliff tops, he was not too worried at first. It was only when the Roman ships sailed closer inshore that Caesar saw this was no welcoming party: the British ranks were bristling with spears and swords.

As the Roman galleys sailed north-east towards Deal, the Britons walked and rode along the cliff-tops, pacing the ships. It was an unnerving sight, and by the time the ships came as close to shore as their size would allow, even the brave Tenth legion, Caesar's favourite, was thoroughly alarmed.

The men were ordered to jump into the water, which was waist-deep. For a moment they hesitated, looking down at the choppy waves. Then, suddenly, the

Caesar surveys the rows of Britons lining the white cliff tops of Dover. As his ship came closer he realized this was no welcoming party; its ranks bristled with swords and spears.

standard-bearer of the Tenth legion shouted at the top of his voice: 'Jump down, men, unless you want the enemy to get your standard! You will not find me failing in my duty to my country or my leader!'

With that he plunged in, and the rest of the Legion, seeing him struggling towards the shore holding above his head the sacred Roman standard jumped in after him.

They were still in the water, weighed down by their arms, with their mailed leather jerkins heavy on their backs, when the British horsemen came riding out into the surf, swinging their swords and shouting terrible battle cries. Behind the horsemen, on the beach, stood more Britons, armed with stones and javelins.

Some of the legionaries, battered from above and slipping on the shingle, collapsed into the water, but enough of them reached the shore to form up in line and take the offensive. In the face of the concerted Roman charge that followed, and the menacing line of Roman javelins, British resistance crumbled and the islanders fled. Without his cavalry, however, Caesar was unable to pursue them.

The next day, realizing the strength of the invaders, the Britons sent a deputation to Caesar. They came rather shamefacedly, led by Commius, Caesar's envoy who told a sorry tale of how he and his horsemen had been set upon and put in chains almost as soon as they had set foot on the island.

The Britons were suitably apologetic, and many of them offered to remain with the Romans as hostages, for the good behaviour of the rest.

Peace, it seemed, had returned, and Caesar's earlier confidence that the conquest of Britain would be a simple matter seemed justified. As the British peasants returned to their fields, the tribal chiefs came to the Roman camp to swear loyalty to Caesar. Meanwhile, the eighty Roman transport ships were anchored, and Caesar awaited the arrival of the ships bringing his cavalry to Britain.

Four days later, the fleet appeared, but almost as soon as they were sighted, a tremendous gale blew up tossing the ships about on the water, snapping their masts, and tearing their sails to shreds. As the fury of the storm mounted the ships were driven back towards France, and by the time night fell all of them had vanished from sight.

It was a terrible blow, but when dawn finally broke, after a night of shrieking winds and torrential rain, an even greater shock awaited Caesar. The beach was littered with the wreckage of his transport vessels, and what remained of them was little more than a pitiful row of storm-battered hulks.

As the Romans surveyed the appalling scene, the British chiefs began to slip away from the camp. They rounded up peasants from the fields, war chariots were made ready, and arms were sharpened. The British, convinced that the Romans were marooned on their unfriendly island, were preparing again for war.

But if they thought the Romans were helpless, they were much mistaken. The Roman legionaries were not only superb fighters, but skilful engineers as well. This would not be the first time they had repaired ships by using the wreckage of those most badly damaged: they could even forge the nails to hold the ships together.

While the men of the Tenth Legion were engaged on this work, their colleagues of the Seventh went foraging for food. From their thick forests of alder and oak, the Britons watched the Romans as they stripped off the jerkins, and began to reap the deserted barley-fields. They watched them for a long time, waiting until the Romans were thoroughly occupied with what they were doing. Then the Britons rushed out of the forest, yelling war-cries and brandishing spears. Within minutes, the Romans, many of whom were unarmed, were surrounded.

Some distance away, in the Roman camp, the sentries saw a huge cloud of dust rise into the sky. Immediately Caesar and a handful of troops stormed out of the camp and raced along the path that led to the fields, buckling on their armour as they went. As Caesar approached, the Britons, certain he had come in force, fled back into the dark recesses of the forest. Limping and bleeding, many of them severely wounded, the foraging party arrived back at their camp when, to add to their misery and Caesar's dismay, the sky poured down torrents of rain for several days.

However, this dreadful weather provided a natural defence for the Romans: it kept the Britons away long enough for some of the repairs to the ships to be completed. Then, as the more seaworthy set off back to Boulogne for more materials, Caesar prepared for the onslaught that would surely come when the weather cleared.

When it did come, the massed chariots which descended on the straight line of Roman soldiers were a formidable sight. 'In chariot fighting,' Caesar wrote in his *Gallic Wars*, 'the Britons begin by driving all over the field hurling javelins. . . . Then, after making their way between the squadrons of their own cavalry, they jump down from the chariots and engage on foot. In the meantime, their charioteers retire a short distance from the battle and place the chariots in such a position that their masters, if hard pressed by numbers, have an easy means of retreat to their own lines.

'Thus, they combine the mobility of cavalry with the staying power of infantry; and by daily training and practice they attain such proficiency that even on a steep incline they are able to control the horses at full gallop, and to check and turn them in a moment. They can run along the chariot-pole, stand on the yoke, and get back into the chariot as quick as lightning.'

Despite their skill, so obviously admired by Caesar, the Britons had to make use of this means of escape to avoid the really determined Roman resistance. The legionaries beat them off, and again the Britons fled to their forests.

By this time, however, Caesar had had enough. The following evening, he packed his soldiers into the galleys and sailed back to France, after less than three weeks in Britain.

Caesar's feelings about this fiasco are not known, but he was careful to send a report to the Senate in Rome which would paint as rosy a picture as possible of what had, in reality, been a near-disaster. He did this so well that the Senate voted a twenty-day 'supplicatio', or period of thanksgiving, for his 'exploit'.

The Senate, along with many other people, got the idea that Caesar's expedition had simply been a dress rehearsal for a full-scale assault, and that a new province was about to be added to the Roman Empire. The notion also spread that Britain was a veritable mine of wealth, waiting only for conquest and pillage by the Romans. As a result, treasure-seekers scrambled to join Caesar's second expedition. They swelled his army to five legions, that is 25,000 men, and 2,000 cavalry.

When the fleet of 800 ships sailed in the summer of 54 B.C., Caesar also took with him an elephant, probably the first ever seen in Britain. This time, the Romans landed on a deserted beach. Some of the newcomers, unaware of the events of the year before, concluded that the sight of so many great ships had frightened the inhabitants into hiding. But Caesar guessed, correctly, that the Britons had decided on another guerrilla war, where their inferior weapons and tactics would be less of a disadvantage than they were in a pitched battle.

A face to face confrontation was what Caesar now desired most. When his scouts took prisoner a few peasants, he learned from them that the British warriors were about ten miles away, on the far side of a river. Though it was nearly midnight, Caesar set off at once, marching by moonlight through the eerie forests and marshes of Kent towards the River Stour.

There was a brief skirmish near the river, but as soon as the Romans began to attack in earnest, the Britons melted away into the trees. The further the Romans advanced the more the Britons retreated, drawing the invaders further and further into the forest.

At last the Romans caught up, and Caesar had just sighted the British rearguard when messengers came riding up with the worst possible news: for the second time, a vicious Channel gale had wrecked Caesar's ships, plucking them from their anchorages and smashing them down upon the shore.

This was not only a strategic blow to Caesar, but a personal one as well. After the disaster the previous year, he himself had supervised the building of ships for this expedition, incorporating in them features which he thought would enable them to ride out the Channel storms. Nature, it seemed, had thwarted him, and there was nothing for it but to abandon his pursuit of the Britons and return to survey the damage.

When he reached the scene he discovered that forty ships were completely wrecked. Others, less badly damaged, were dragged up on the beach, and for ten days, behind closely guarded fortifications, the Romans worked hard to repair the ships.

When, at long last, the work was completed, Caesar found that the Britons had again put to good use the breathing space given them by their unpredictable weather. The various tribes had set aside their long-standing rivalries, and had combined forces under one leader. He was Cassivellaunus, King of the Catuvellauni, whose kingdom was in the neighbourhood of St. Albans, some twenty miles from where London now stands.

British tactics, however, remained the same, as Caesar discovered when a horde of their chariots swooped down on his soldiers while they were digging trenches. The chariots created havoc among the unarmed Romans, and then sped back into the forest as quickly as they had come.

Caesar now realized that a set-piece battle against such nimble adversaries was out of the question, and so he ordered his men to dig in. Then he waited behind earth ramparts bristling with wooden stakes for Cassivellaunus to attack.

Cassivellaunus let him wait. From his fortified forest camp on the other side of the River Thames, the British leader preferred to send out raiding parties and stage ambushes, rather than come out and fight a battle.

British chariots crash over the top of the 'tortoise'. When hard-pressed, the Romans closed ranks and protected themselves by overlapping their shields and crouching beneath them.

At last, with summer fast fading into autumn, Caesar took the initiative, only to find that the Britons had barricaded the Thames by driving stakes into the river-bed at the crossing place. This problem was solved when the Romans clothed their elephant in an armour of iron scales, and put on its back a tower full of archers and slingers. As the great beast lumbered into the river, with a shower of arrows and stones pouring down from the tower, the terrified Britons turned and fled.

However, although they had crossed the river, the Romans found the situation no better. Cassivellaunus refused to stand and fight, still preferring his hit-and-run tactics.

Finally, Caesar tried subversion. He had in his camp the son of a British Chief who had recently been conquered by Cassivellaunus. Cracks soon appeared in the alliance of tribes when Caesar promised to restore this young Briton to his kingdom. Some of the smaller tribes deserted Cassivellaunus, who, in his growing isolation, persuaded the four Kings of Kent to attack Caesar's base camp and so draw the Roman leaders away to defend it.

The plan failed, but Caesar eagerly seized his chance when Cassivellaunus asked for a truce. Caesar negotiated the treaty imperiously, almost as if he had won a victory, but he did not waste time with precautions to ensure Cassivellaunus kept his promises to abide by it. Leaving the inhospitable island and the elusive foe it contained was Caesar's only thought.

With autumn gales already blowing round the British coast, with the winds whipping up dangerously choppy seas, Caesar once more crammed his soldiers in his ships and sailed for Gaul.

He never returned to Britain, for a succession of circumstances prevented him – unrest in Gaul, a civil war against Pompey (his son-in-law), his entanglement with Cleopatra in Egypt, and finally his assassination in 44 B.C.

Britain remained undisturbed for nearly 100 years until A.D. 43 when the Roman Emperor Claudius, hungry for new conquests, mounted his invasion. It succeeded, and was the beginning of four centuries of Roman rule, a rule which left an imprint still evident in Britain today.

The greatest
Discoverer of them all
Christopher Columbus stumbles
on the New World

On 13 August 1476 an armed convoy from Genoa
was on its way to Northern Europe. The convoy,
carrying a cargo of great value, was sailing west along
the south coast of Portugal, when suddenly it was
attacked by French warships. The two fleets battled
furiously throughout the day, and by nightfall three of
the Genoese and four of the French ships had gone
down. From the deck of one of the sinking Genoese a
twenty-five-year-old wool dealer jumped into the sea,
and, although wounded, managed to grab hold of a
floating oar. By alternately pushing it ahead and rest-
ing on it he reached the shore, six miles away. It was a
miraculous escape from death, and the lucky young
man was convinced that he had been spared by God
to perform works of great importance. Five hundred
years later his name is as famous as any in the history
of mankind – Christopher Columbus.

Villagers from nearby Lagos came to Columbus's
rescue as he dragged himself up on to the shore, and
after treating his injuries and feeding him they sent
him off to Lisbon where, he told them, his brother
Bartholomew was living. This dramatic escape from
certain death, and the meeting with Bartholomew are
practically the first things we know about the man who

was to discover the New World. He claimed to have been born in Genoa, and it is likely that he was descended from a Spanish-Jewish family that had settled there a few generations earlier. Yet by the time Christopher was born, probably in 1451, the Columbus family was very definitely Christian. His father was a weaver, and Columbus would have been brought up in the same trade, although he claimed later that he began his sailing career when he was only fourteen. If so, it would have been as an apprentice trader, not as a working seaman. When he was swept up on to the Portuguese coast he certainly would have known a great deal more about the wool trade than about navigation.

The Lisbon that Christopher Columbus so fortunately stumbled into was, at that time, the most exciting and adventurous city in Europe. It was the centre of a great quest – the search for a sea route to the Indies.

The Indies, which was the term applied to all of Asia from India to Japan, exerted an almost hypnotic attraction for the Europeans of the 15th century. Men dreamed of the East – the fabled lands of gold and silver, silks and spices, precious stones and perfumes. Year after year these exotic wares trickled into Europe, brought in caravans thousands of miles across the wastes of Central Asia to Constantinople, and distributed from there by Mediterranean merchants. Because they passed from hand to hand half-way round the world, these goods were extraordinarily costly to Europeans. Worse still, in 1453, Constantinople, the eastern stronghold of Christianity, fell to the infidel Turk. The entire trade was now at the mercy of a deadly enemy. If only there were some way of getting to the source of these riches by sea, and cutting out all the middlemen, particularly the hated Turks! Any king, any country that could make that dream come true would make an immense fortune, almost overnight.

And there was much more at stake than just money. Christian Europe had never recovered from the disgraceful failure of the Crusades. It was humiliating to live with the knowledge that the Holy Land was in Turkish hands. As the European countries emerged from the Middle Ages, confident, wealthy, and proud, it became an obsession with them to right this intolerable wrong. Furthermore, the scheme appeared practical because it was believed that somewhere in the Far East there existed a powerful Christian nation ruled by the mighty Prester John. If the European Christians could only link forces with this Prester John, together they could drive the Turks out of the Holy Land.

Of course, Prester John and his Christian kingdom were a myth, but to the contemporaries of Columbus they were vividly real.

The truth of the matter was that Europeans, even the most learned Europeans, knew very little about Asia. Practically everything they did know they had read in the famous travel book by Marco Polo, a Venetian who had journeyed as far as Cathay (China) towards the end of the 13th century. His book was one of the very first ever printed, and it was enormously popular. Marco Polo had seen at first hand the fabulous wealth of the Chinese Emperors. Not only that, he wrote fascinating accounts of an even richer kingdom that lay some 1,500 miles off the coast of China. This one he had never laid eyes on, but he repeated its name – Zipangu (Japan).

Although almost everybody wanted to get to the Indies, it was the Portuguese who were doing something about it. Their plan was a very straightforward and sensible one. It was to sail down the unexplored coast of Africa until the southern tip was reached. Nobody knew where that was, but Africa had to end somewhere. Having got round the tip it would be a simple matter to sail across the Indian Ocean until the magical Indies came into sight.

In 1438 Prince Henry the Navigator founded a nautical centre for that very purpose, and to Lisbon flocked merchants, sea-captains, map-makers, astronomers, indeed all those who shared the dream. Year after year Portuguese ships pushed further and further south along the African coast. Portuguese captains discovered the Azores, the Cape Verde Islands, and colonized the Madeira group. Ships returned to Lisbon laden with ivory, gold dust, slaves, and tales of more and more land to the south.

It was against this background, into a Lisbon seething with adventure and discovery, that Christopher Columbus came on the scene.

His brother Bartholomew promptly got him a job in the chart-making establishment that he himself worked for. Christopher leapt to the task, learned the skills quickly, and soon the two brothers set up a thriving business of their own.

But Christopher Columbus was not content merely to make charts of other people's discoveries. He had schemes of his own for reaching the Indies, and to have any chance of fulfilling them he must first learn more about navigation, and he must get this knowledge first-hand. In the very year he arrived in Lisbon he signed on Portuguese merchant ships, and over the

The flagship *Santa Maria,* which Columbus himself commanded. Although it would not have been more than ninety feet long *(Pinta* and *Nina* were even smaller), it was fast and seaworthy.

next few years he made voyages as far north as Iceland, as far west as the Azores (the westernmost bits of land known), and as far south as the Gold Coast. He also had the good fortune to marry into one of the foremost families in Portugal, a family well-connected with the whole business of maritime exploration and trade.

At some point during these chart-making and voyaging days an idea of great importance for the future of mankind began to take shape in Columbus's mind. In the long run the attempts to get to the Indies by sailing round Africa and across the Indian Ocean were bound to succeed. Columbus knew that and everybody knew that. It was only a matter of time. But surely that was the difficult way to go about it. Why not sail due *west*? Now the idea of reaching the east by sailing west was not an original one. Learned men ever since the days of the Ancient Greeks had believed that the world was a sphere, and by the time Columbus seized upon the notion only the ignorant and the prejudiced thought the world was flat. If the world were a sphere then it would make perfect sense to sail west to get to the Indies.

At least it made sense in theory. There was only one snag. Those who knew most about the subject, namely the expert navigators and astronomers who surrounded the throne of Portugal, considered that such a journey to the Indies was impossible because the distance was too great. No ship could sail that far without stopping for provisions. And they were right! We must remember that nobody in southern Europe had the slightest inkling of the existence of America. The discovery of Vinland (the east coast of what is now Canada and the northern United States) by Scandinavian adventurers, almost 500 years earlier, was either un-known or forgotten in southern Europe. The journey west would mean sailing out of sight of land right round to the other side of the world, and no ship of the time could possibly have managed to do it. Further-more, one didn't have to sail very far west of Lisbon to realize that the North Atlantic was a thoroughly un-inviting stretch of water to experiment with. The seas ran cold, dark, and rough; the winds were uncertain, and often wild and destructive. It was not for nothing that the Atlantic was known as the Sea of Darkness. Sailors, to a man, preferred to give it a wide berth.

Columbus, however, was not deterred for a moment by the doubts of experts and the fears of sailors. As far as he was concerned all these experts were wrong. He had figured it all out, and the Ocean Sea (the name by which the entire world ocean was known – Euro-peans knew nothing of the Pacific) was not that wide. In fact it wasn't very wide at all. By picking and choosing among various estimates of the size of the globe, he arrived at the conclusion that Japan was well under 3,000 miles due west of the Canary Islands, and China another 1,500 or so further on. Not only that, he even managed to lay his hands on a map drawn by the famous Florentine astronomer, Paolo Toscanelli, who *showed* Japan and China sitting out there exactly where he said they were.

In fact it is over 10,000 miles from the Canary Is-lands to Japan! By his wildly inaccurate calculations Columbus had placed Japan and China where the east coast of America is. If the Indies were that close then the journey *was* possible, and he, Christopher Colum-bus, was the man to do it.

It wasn't enough, of course, that he was convinced,

or that a wise man of Florence agreed. The journey would require men, ships, and money; in short, it needed the backing of a king.

Gathering all his evidence together Columbus, in 1484, approached the King of Portugal. King John II was a nephew of Prince Henry the Navigator and had inherited his uncle's passion for exploration. He listened politely as Columbus poured out his fantastic scheme – complete with charts, obscure mathematical calculations, and even biblical quotations about the size of the ocean. King John, sceptical but interested, sent the plan to his expert advisers.

They promptly turned it down. The experts were well aware that all these calculations flung at them by Columbus were more fantasy than fact. All his talk about 'Land to the West' was a mere pipe dream. The way to the East was to sail east.

Thoroughly disgusted, Columbus promptly made plans to leave Portugal. Somebody somewhere was going to sponsor him and he didn't much care who it was. He dispatched Bartholomew to the Courts of England and France to try and drum up enthusiasm for his project, and himself set off for Spain. His wife had recently died, leaving him with a young son, Diego, so with Diego by his side Columbus boarded a ship bound for Palos, a small port on the south coast of Spain not far from the Portuguese border. They headed straight for the neighbouring Franciscan monastery because these monasteries had a reputation for taking on 'Boarders', and something had to be done about looking after Diego. It was a lucky move.

One of the monks, Antonio de Marchena, immediately struck up a conversation with Columbus. Marchena was an extremely learned man and he listened to this stranger with growing interest. As Columbus rambled on and on about his great scheme Marchena became entranced. He offered to look after Diego's education and promptly introduced Columbus to the man who was most likely to help him – the Duke of Medina Celi, a Spanish noble and an important ship-owner in Cadiz. Medina Celi greeted Columbus with enthusiasm, and would have backed the venture himself had he not realized that so momentous an enterprise should really be in the hands of the monarchs of Spain. He recommended Columbus to King Ferdinand and Queen Isabella.

Nine months later, in the spring of 1486, the Queen sent for Columbus. Isabella, a tremendously able and far-seeing monarch, found this strange man very much to her liking. If he was slightly fanatical and utterly obsessed with his one great idea at least it was a noble idea, and a man of such blinding faith and sincerity was not to be scoffed at. The fact that her husband, Ferdinand, was sceptical did not deter her. She explained to Columbus, however, that, attractive though the proposition was, it was out of the question for the time being. Spain was entering the final stages of a mighty effort to drive the Moors from their last bastion in Europe, and not a penny could be spared from the Treasury until that purpose had been accomplished. In the meantime, Columbus was invited to stay close by, and provided with funds to live on until such time as the matter could be given greater attention. Columbus, enormously pleased at finally being taken seriously, agreed to wait. And he waited for six years.

It was the most frustrating period in his life; forced to sit around waiting for a war to finish before he could get on with the business of discovering 'Land to the West'.

Finally, about Christmas 1491, Columbus was summoned to the Queen. Granada, the last Moorish stronghold, was about to fall and Isabella had not forgotten her promise. Although the advisers to the Queen had spent the entire six years attempting to stop such a mad scheme, she had made up her mind. All that was left was to settle the terms.

Then, right on the threshold of victory, Columbus dropped a bomb-shell. He calmly delivered the terms under which he would sail west for the throne of Spain.

He, Columbus, would become Admiral of the Ocean Sea and be granted all the privileges of the highest noble in Spain. His heirs would inherit this title and these privileges forever. He and his heirs forever would be Viceroys and Governors of all the islands and continents that he discovered. He and his heirs forever would receive ten per cent of all gold, silver, precious stones, spices, and whatever else of value should be acquired anywhere at any time within his admiralty. There was more, but it is doubtful whether anyone was paying serious attention at this point. The demands were ridiculous and were promptly rejected.

Columbus, without a moment's hesitation, turned his back on the Court, saddled his mule and headed for France, where he had heard Bartholomew was finally making some progress with Charles VIII.

As he set out, with six years of unrelenting toil and the greatest adventure in human history about to go down the drain, the Court of Isabella was in a turmoil. One of the wealthiest and most influential men in

Spain, Luis de Santangel, approached the Queen. Columbus, he argued, *must* not be allowed to take his plan to another country. Somebody, sooner or later, was going to back this wild man and it had better be Spain. Furthermore, extravagant though Columbus's demands were, they should be agreed to because they all hinged on a successful venture. If he found nothing, the King and Queen need give him nothing. If, on the other hand, Columbus were right and untold riches were awaiting him just over the horizon, ten per cent and a few titles was a cheap enough price to pay. What on earth could be lost except the money needed for ships and provisions? And as for that, he, Santangel, would finance the project if necessary!

This argument, backed by so generous an offer, carried the day. A messenger swiftly overtook Columbus, who was six miles away – slowly making his way to France – and summoned him back to the Queen.

So it was that on 17 April 1492 the famous contract between Christopher Columbus and the Sovereigns of Spain was formally signed and witnessed. Known, fittingly enough, as the Capitulation, it gave Columbus everything he asked for. The man of vision, of iron-willed determination, had finally won through, and on his own terms.

Like a man possessed, Columbus now threw himself into the task of organizing the expedition. Ships, men, provisions, all had to be got ready, and there wasn't a moment to lose. Only a year earlier, the great Portuguese mariner Bartholomew Dias had sailed proudly back to Lisbon after successfully rounding the tip of Africa. The way to the Indies was now wide open and the Portuguese might press on across the Indian Ocean at any moment.

Palos, the little town Columbus had arrived at six years before, was chosen as the port of embarkation. Three small ships were selected: *Santa Maria, Pinta,* and *Nina*. The largest of them, *Santa Maria*, would not have been more than ninety feet long, but they were all strong, fast, seaworthy craft. Columbus decided to command *Santa Maria* himself, and for the others he recruited Martin Alonso Pinzón, one of the most experienced mariners in all of Spain, and his brother Vincente Pinzón.

Without the support of the illustrious Pinzón family Columbus would have found it practically impossible to round up crews for the voyage. The prospect of sailing out into the unknown did not much appeal to the local sailors, but if Martín Pinzón was going maybe there was something in it. And the pay was good. Ninety men duly volunteered.

By the evening of 2 August 1492 everything was ready. The men took leave of their families and went to their ships. In the early hours of the morning of the 3rd Columbus boarded his flagship, *Santa Maria*, and gave the order to cast off. As the dawn came the three small ships bravely struck out on the greatest voyage of all time.

Christopher Columbus, now in the forty-second year of his life, was finally on the way to his 'Land to the West'. The desperate years of pleading, arguing, and waiting were behind him. He was no longer poor, and his affairs were in order. Diego was conveniently placed as a page to Queen Isabella's son, Prince Juan. A second son, Fernando, was to stay with his mother Beatriz Enriquez, with whom Columbus had set up home during his long wait in Spain. There was nothing to stand between him and the great destiny he believed in so completely. Nothing, that is, except an unknown ocean.

The first part of the journey went according to plan. The Canary Islands were reached within a week, and after taking on fresh provisions and attending to some minor repairs on *Pinta,* the tiny fleet set out, as Columbus put in his logbook, 'West, nothing to the north, nothing to the south.' It was now 6 September. By the 9th the last bit of land disappeared from view. They were now travelling in completely uncharted waters. Day after day they pushed forward, swept along by the trade wind. The sailing conditions were superb, sunny days, clear starlit nights, and a steady wind. Columbus could not have asked for more. The miles skipped by, almost 1,200 in the first ten days, as Columbus happily recorded in his journal. With great cunning, however, he began keeping two logbooks – one with the actual distance travelled each day, and the other with a false mileage, considerably less than was actually covered. These were the figures he gave out to the men – so that they would not realize how far they were getting away from the safety of Spain!

Columbus realized that as the days went by without sign of land the men would become anxious. He was right. Despite the false figures they were given, the sailors started to become restless after three weeks. How on earth were they ever going to get back home if they just kept sailing on and on with the wind steadily behind them? Another week went by and still no sign of land. After thirty-one days panic began to grip the crew. Columbus did his best to calm them but mutiny was in the air. By 9 October the situation was desperate as Columbus tried to reason with the terrified crew, pointing out the flocks of birds passing over the ship, surely a sign that land was near. The next day the wind blew harder as the ships sailed on, their course altered southward to follow the flights of birds. On the 11th branches of trees were seen floating in the water – an unmistakable sign of land – and flocks of birds became more numerous. The mutinuous whispers died down. The wind blew even harder and the ships raced on faster and faster. As the evening drew on excitement was in the air. The Sovereigns had offered a reward of a year's pay to the first man who sighted land and every eye was glued to the horizon. Each ship strained to be in front, to get the first glimpse.

Pinta hurtled along in the lead, with *Nina* and *Santa Maria* pressing close behind. At 10 p.m. Columbus saw a light, or thought he did. Moments later others too claimed to see the light, but it was an illusion and after a few minutes it could no longer be seen.

Midnight came and went. Then, at 2 a.m., Rodrigo de Triana, the lookout on *Pinta* sent up the cry. *Tierra! Tierra!* Land! Land! Cannon fire roared from *Pinta*. It was land. There was no doubt this time as *Pinta* slowed down and waited for the others to catch up. It was 12 October 1492. Without knowing it, a group of Spanish sailors led by a Genoese visionary had made a great discovery. They had discovered the New World.

The ships hove to overnight and at dawn they were in full view of a small island in the Bahamas. They sailed along the coast looking for an opening through the reef, and by noon they found one. As they edged towards the shore they could see naked people of a copper brown colour gathering, following their movements. Admiral Columbus (as he now styled himself – after all he had found 'Land to the West') went ashore in a small boat followed by the other two captains, Martín

A map showing the route sailed by Columbus on his first voyage; from Spain (Spagna) south to the Canary Islands and west to San Salvador; then homewards from Hispaniola (Haiti) to Lisbon.

and Vincente Pinzón. There, on the white shore, they knelt in prayer giving thanks for the success of the journey. Columbus then rose to his feet and took possession of the land for the King and Queen of Spain, naming it San Salvador.

Happy though he was at reaching land Columbus was decidedly puzzled as he looked around at his new kingdom. By his reckoning he should be in Japan. Who on earth were these naked, golden-skinned savages who approached so timidly? They were hardly the sophisticated, jewel-bedecked Orientals that Marco Polo had talked so much about!

At any rate these natives were friendly. Columbus gave them some red caps, glass beads, and assorted trinkets and they were delighted. Straightaway they began swimming out to the boats, bringing parrots, spears, and balls of cotton thread. Before long a thriving trade was in full swing – but it was not the sort of trade Columbus had in mind. It was plain to see that these poor people were not going to fill the vaults of Spain with gold and the warehouses with spices. The

King and Queen were not going to be overjoyed by a cargo of parrots.

On closer scrutiny, however, some of these natives – 'Indians', Columbus called them, serene in the belief that he had reached the Indies – had gold rings in their noses. The Indians were only too happy to oblige when they were made to understand, through sign-language, that their guests were keen to know the source of this metal. They pointed to the south and the west, where, they claimed, there were many more islands. After a couple of days exploring San Salvador, or Guanahani as the natives called their home, Columbus set sail in the direction indicated, detaining six Indians as guides. Sure enough there were plenty of islands, but they were much the same as the first one; flat, jungle-covered bits of land inhabited by natives who were decidedly friendly but disturbingly poor. Columbus noticed maize (completely unknown to Europeans), yams, even woven hammocks, but no gold except for the little pieces that the natives wore.

Back and forth from island to island the Spaniards criss-crossed. But everywhere they went it was the same story. The gold always came from some other place, just round the corner. Finally they stumbled on Cuba, the first big island. But it still did not look like Japan was supposed to look. Here in Cuba, however, the trail warmed up. The natives spoke of a place in the interior called Cubanacan. Cubanacan, they promised, was where the gold came from. The Admiral who had brought with him a letter of introduction to the Great Khan of China, pricked up his ears. Cubanacan, he decided, meant *El Gran Can* ('the Great Khan'), and he promptly sent along a few hand-picked men to present his compliments. Instead of an imperial Chinese city they discovered a miserable little village of palm-thatched huts. Discouraged, they tramped back to the coast, encountering on the way 'many people who were going to their villages, with a firebrand in the hand, and herbs to drink the smoke thereof!' It was the first European encounter with a strange practice that they themselves would adopt before long – smoking tobacco.

Tempers were getting short among the Spaniards as this fruitless search for gold dragged on. Suddenly, without any warning or permission, Martín Pinzón set off in *Pinta*, following his own hunch about where all the gold might be.

Columbus, in *Santa Maria*, and the loyal Vincente Pinzón in *Nina* sailed eastward along the coast of Cuba, across open water, and ran smack into Hispaniola. And here, at last, they found signs of the elusive gold. The natives were still almost completely naked, but they wore lots of golden ornaments. And, as usual, they were happy to part with them for little bells and red caps.

The Spaniards were now certain that they had struck it rich and Columbus was just about to launch an expedition into the interior when disaster struck. Just after midnight on Christmas morning *Santa Maria* slid onto a coral reef and slowly began to break up. There were no casualties but the ship was a complete loss. Columbus, as usual, interpreted the disaster as a blessing in disguise. It was a sign from Heaven that he should found a colony in Hispaniola. A small, fortified camp was immediately built, mainly from the timbers of *Santa Maria*, and thirty-nine men volunteered to stay behind and form the little colony, which Columbus named Villa de la Navidad (Christmas Town). The Admiral left orders that the island be explored and the natives well-treated, then set sail with the remaining men, in *Nina*. But he was no longer looking for islands. He had found what he wanted. Hispaniola might not be Japan, but it was a rich island off the coast of China, and he had enough gold to prove it. He would even take half a dozen Indians along for good measure. It was time to get back to Spain with the good news, even if *Nina* had to go it alone.

On 4 January 1493 the homeward journey began. They had sailed only two days when another ship appeared on the horizon, sailing towards them. It was *Pinta!* Martin Pinzón came aboard and gave an account of himself. It seemed he had heard rumours of an island where the natives collected gold in the dead of night, by candlelight of all things, and he had set off to see if there was anything to back it up. Needless to say there wasn't, but he had then landed on another part of the coast of Hispaniola and found plenty of gold – just like Columbus. Reports of the destruction of *Santa Maria* had reached his ears and he was on his way to lend a hand. The quarrel was patched up and the two ships headed for Spain.

They very nearly didn't make it. All went well for about a month, until they were nearing the Azores. There they suddenly found themselves caught up in one of the most brutal winters in European history. Gales lashed the tiny ships, they were swept apart and lost sight of each other, and *Nina* very nearly capsized. In desperation, lest they all drown and his great discovery perish with them, Columbus wrote down an account of the journey, sealed it in a keg, and threw it overboard. The keg has never been recovered, but fortunately it wasn't needed. *Nina* finally stumbled into the shelter of the Azores.

After a brush with the Portuguese authorities – who suspected them of poaching on Portuguese discoveries in West Africa – Columbus and his men set off once more.

They sailed right into the teeth of a hurricane, and once again Columbus proved what a superb seaman and leader he really was, keeping a rock-steady nerve, and putting heart into the terrified crew when all seemed lost. After two weeks of sheer hell the coast of Portugal came in sight, and although Portugal was about the last place on earth Columbus wanted to land he had no choice. He simply couldn't chance pushing on in such terrible weather. On 4 March the battered little ship limped into the outer port of Lisbon.

The crew rushed ashore, telling everyone in sight of the marvellous discovery. But Columbus was decidedly worried. What would King John think? After all Columbus had proved him wrong, practically made a fool of him, and the King might well take revenge on him. But it was too late for that. Whatever King John felt about it, the news was out and he might as well be a gracious loser. He sent for Columbus, congratulated him on his success, and sent him on his way.

At midday on 15 March *Nina* dropped anchor off Palos, the very harbour they had left 224 days before. Crowds rushed forward to greet them. The men tumbled off the ship into the arms of their families and fellow-townsmen. The heroes had returned. And to make the day complete *Pinta* turned up just a few hours later. But the terrible journey had finished Martín Pinzón. He went directly home, took to his bed, and died. Not so Columbus. The triumph was his and he meant to savour it.

A procession was formed – Columbus, his officers, and six bewildered Indians – and they started out for Barcelona and the King and Queen. All along the route crowds flocked to see Columbus and his amazing entourage. Cheers filled the air as the proud Discoverer made his way slowly north.

Finally they reached their destination. Columbus strode into the great hall where Ferdinand and Isabella were awaiting him. Those present said he moved with the dignity and nobility of a Roman senator. His grey hair swept back, his face tanned and weather-beaten, he approached his Sovereigns. He was no longer a wild-eyed dreamer, a man pleading for an audience. The King and Queen did him the supreme honour of rising from their thrones to greet him, just as though he were a foreign monarch, and when he knelt to kiss their hands they commanded him to rise and be seated on the Queen's right.

They listened enthralled as he poured out his exciting story and displayed his wondrous specimens – parrots, Indians, tobacco, and of course gold.

Columbus was the man of the hour. There was no honour too great for him and the Sovereigns did not begrudge him his moment of triumph. He had discovered his 'Land to the West' – whatever it was – to the greater glory of Spain, and the greater glory of Ferdinand and Isabella. He would henceforth be known as Don Christopher Columbus, Admiral of the Ocean Seas, Viceroy of the Indies.

But that is not the end of the story of Christopher Columbus. Three more times he sailed to 'his' Indies,

Columbus returns in triumph. Crowds flocked to see the great Discoverer as his procession moved slowly north from Palos to Barcelona and the Court of Isabella and Ferdinand.

round and round the islands, always looking for the way through to China. Although it became increasingly obvious to everyone else that these Indies were nowhere near China, and were in fact a 'New World', Columbus never wavered in his belief that he was somewhere just off the coast of the Orient. If he could only find a way through! At one point he even touched the coast of South America, but that wasn't what he was looking for. He was looking for China, and of course he never found it.

These later voyages of Columbus are scarred by tragedy. When, on the second trip he returned to his much boasted-about colony in Hispaniola he found it in ruins and the men he had left behind all massacred. It came out that these Spaniards had horribly abused the hospitality of the natives and had paid for it with their lives. This was just the beginning of one of the most sordid chapters in history. Although Columbus had always insisted on treating the Indians well, few Spaniards shared his concern. The white men had been looked upon as gods when they arrived in this New World but they were not to justify this faith. Over the next fifty years millions of the original inhabitants of these new lands perished, worked to death in the gold mines, and frequently slaughtered in cold blood, often just for amusement.

Although Columbus was a great explorer he was an inefficient governor, and the situation in the new Spanish possessions rapidly drifted out of control. Disaffection spread among the new settlers, much of it aimed at him, and after the third voyage he was recalled in disgrace, brought back to Spain in chains. He had fallen on evil times, and although he was promptly released by the King and Queen his days of real influence were over.

After returning from his fourth and final voyage he devoted his remaining years to a hopeless attempt to re-assert all the privileges and honours that had been steadily whittled away. But when his staunchest ally, Queen Isabella, died in 1504, he must have realized that his was a lost cause. From then until he died he concentrated his efforts on having his son Diego made Viceroy of the Indies.

In this he succeeded. Diego became governor of Hispaniola in 1509, but Columbus did not live to see it. His great strength, drained by these last years of bitter frustration, finally gave out and he died on 19 May 1506. By then the seas were crowded with other explorers, discovering 'his' islands, gathering up 'his' honours, gaining 'his' wealth. A new era had begun, and the man who had started the whole adventure was soon almost forgotten. But today nearly 500 years later, when we think of the courage and daring of early explorers we think of the greatest of them all, Christopher Columbus.

A fraud that rocked the throne of France

The affair of the diamond necklace

It was on a May morning in 1770 that the thirty-six-year-old Bishop of Strasbourg, Prince Louis de Rohan, stood on the steps of his Cathedral to welcome to France, a fifteen-year-old Hapsburg Princess called Marie Antoinette. She was the daughter of Maria Theresa, Empress of Austria, and was to marry the Dauphin Louis, grandson of King Louis XV and heir to the French throne. Rohan was handsome, charming, and belonged to a family of enormous wealth, prestige, and court influence. She was remarkably pretty, with a shallow, frivolous nature. Fifteen years later the pair became embroiled in the scandal of the age, a scandal that Napoleon later described as one of the causes of the French Revolution. It was the 'Affair of the Diamond Necklace'.

It was not long before their paths crossed again. In 1772 Rohan was appointed French Ambassador to Austria. During his service there the Empress Maria Theresa took an intense dislike to him, so it is little wonder that when Marie Antoinette became Queen of France in 1774, Rohan found himself dismissed, exiled to his estates in Alsace, and with little prospect of advancing his career. A ray of hope appeared in 1777 when, despite the Queen's protests, he was appointed

Grand Almoner, in charge of the royal charitable funds, and a Cardinal. Such promotion whetted his ambition to follow in the footsteps of two other great Cardinals, Richelieu and Mazarin, and to become, like them, principal minister to the Crown.

In 1780 there entered on the scene another actor in the drama, the Sicilian-born Count Alessandro di Cagliostro, astrologer, hypnotist, faith-healer and alchemist. His imposing presence, spectacular style of living, and unique manner of speaking (a mixture of French and Italian with occasional Arabic phrases thrown in for effect) had gained him an international reputation – and considerable wealth. The gullible Cardinal Rohan fell completely under his spell and would take no important decision without consulting him.

But somebody far more dangerous also had her eyes fixed on the Cardinal – a beautiful, ambitious, and utterly unscrupulous young woman named Jeanne de Valois. She claimed to be descended, through an illegitimate branch, from the royal house of Valois and had married, in 1780, one Marc Antoine Nicolas de La Motte, who had adopted the title of Count. It was therefore as Countess de La Motte that she appeared before the Cardinal three years later – penniless but determined to use her title as a means of social advancement. In a rash moment Rohan had revealed to her that he was deeply in debt and desperately anxious to regain the Queen's goodwill. The Countess saw a golden opportunity to use him for her own selfish purposes.

Already captivated by her charm, Rohan accepted her fabricated story of being the Queen's close confidante who was prepared to act as go-between in restoring

71

An 18th-century print of the magnificent Palace of Versailles. It was against this background of splendour and extravagance that the greatest scandal of the age was played out.

him to royal favour. When she told him that the Queen had agreed to receive a letter from him pleading his cause, he fell headlong into the trap. Back came a reply on scented, gilt-edged paper, signed by Marie Antoinette herself, forgiving him. More letters followed, hinting at further advancement. The deliriously happy Cardinal was now encouraged in his petitions by Cagliostro, who prophesied his eventual success.

The Countess, in fact, had never even spoken to the Queen, whom she envied and despised, and the signature on the letters was being forged by a former cavalry colleague of her husband, an unprincipled adventurer named Marc Antoine Rétaux de Villette. Yet it must have seemed feasible to the Cardinal that Countess de La Motte was the very type of companion who would have appealed to the Queen, who was bored with her husband, extravagantly fond of jewels and clothes, and known to spend most of her time at balls, at the theatre or opera, and at the gambling tables. Indeed, Marie Antoinette had been frequently warned by both her mother, Maria Theresa, and her brother, Joseph, against such indiscreet behaviour, and she was already hated and derided by most of her subjects.

Events began to take a more sinister turn when the Countess decided the time had come to extract money from the credulous Cardinal. One day she presented him with a letter from the Queen requesting a loan from the royal alms funds to cover her debts – 60,000 francs, a considerable sum. When Cagliostro advised him to comply, Rohan handed the 'loan' to the faithful intermediary, the Countess de La Motte. Some days later she stationed Rohan in the Hall of Mirrors at Versailles and managed to persuade him that the

Marie Antoinette, Queen of France, and the innocent victim of the fraud. Nevertheless she became the target of savage ridicule, and her unpopularity greatly increased.

Queen had nodded to him as a sign of royal approbation. Soon there came another request for 60,000 francs then another for 30,000 francs. The last was paid out of Rohan's own dwindling private funds. Still he suspected nothing, while Paris observed the growing splendour and shameless displays of wealth paraded by the Count and Countess de La Motte, thanks to their windfall.

The Cardinal could not understand why the Queen showed no further public sign of her favour, and his restlessness led the Countess to devise another elaborate hoax. Explaining that the Queen could not afford to acknowledge him publicly, but was prepared to do so privately, the Countess arranged for the Cardinal to present himself one July night in 1784 at the Grove of Venus in the gardens of the Palace of Versailles. A figure appeared, cloaked in black and white and escorted by the Countess – assuredly the Queen herself. She pressed a rose into his hand, murmuring 'You know what this means', and the overwhelmed Cardinal fell at her feet, just able to kiss her slipper before the meeting was abruptly ended. The part of the Queen had in fact been played by a young courtesan, Mlle Nicole d'Oliva, hired by the La Mottes because of her striking resemblance to Marie Antoinette, and paid 1,500 francs for the night's work.

The really astonishing fraud, however, was yet to come. Countess de La Motte discovered the existence of a magnificent diamond necklace, fashioned by the court jewellers, Boehmer and Bassenge, for the mistress of Louis XV, Madame du Barry. It was a gorgeous piece of jewellery valued at 1,800,000 francs, a colossal sum. Now that the King was dead and du Barry out of favour, Boehmer and Bassenge were without a buyer, and considerably out of pocket. On the birth of the Queen's first child in 1778, they had offered it to her for sale. Marie Antoinette had exclaimed, 'At that price, we have less need of a necklace than a ship of the line!' The Countess approached Rohan, and informed him that the Queen really did want the necklace, but wanted it purchased in secret, so that she would not be attacked for extravagance. Would Rohan negotiate on her behalf? He was, of course, only too happy to be of service, especially when he was shown her written authorization – forged by Villette.

When the Countess introduced Rohan as a potential buyer, the jewellers were naturally overjoyed. They

The fabulous diamond necklace. It was broken up,
smuggled out to London, and discreetly sold.

were even more delighted when they learned who their
client really was. They too were fooled by Villette's
forged signature, and knocked 200,000 francs off the
price as a special favour. The contract was signed on
29 January 1785. Payment was to be made quarterly
over a two-year period, the first instalment of 400,000
francs falling due on the following 30 July.

On 1 February the necklace was delivered to the
Cardinal, who that night conveyed it to the Countess
and watched her hand it over to the Queen's confidential 'valet' (the faithful Villette once more). The
necklace was never seen again.

The Queen had supposedly requested delivery for a
ceremony the next day, and Rohan was puzzled when
she failed to wear the necklace either on that day or on
any occasion during the following weeks. The Count
meanwhile had broken up the necklace, taken it to
London, and disposed of the stones, confident that
they could not be traced.

Suspicion was first aroused when the date for the initial payment arrived with the Queen pleading 'slight embarrassment', and asking for an extension and then a price reduction. Eventually Boehmer sent a letter directly to the Queen, congratulating her on possessing the jewels, and applying for payment. The Queen assumed he was mad (she had been informed that the necklace had been sold in Constantinople) and burned the letter. But when she obtained a copy of the 'contract', and saw the forged signature, the deception was revealed. The jewellers were aghast at having been tricked, and when Rohan approached the Queen's lady-in-waiting for the overdue money he, too, was horrified to learn that he had been the victim of a cruel hoax. The King arrested his Cardinal in the Hall of Mirrors on 15 August, and had him thrown into the Bastille. There he was joined three days later by the Countess, and later by Nicole d'Oliva and Cagliostro, who was arrested for high treason together with his innocent wife.

At the preliminary hearings there were dramatic confrontations between the Cardinal, the Countess, and Cagliostro. The Countess made up a story about a love affair between Rohan and the Queen and his theft of the necklace, but was worn down by a succession of hostile witnesses. When Villette was arrested in Geneva he revealed the true story, while positive proof of the Count's disposal of the diamonds was obtained from a firm of London jewellers.

Public support was strong for the Cardinal and scorn for the Queen louder than ever when the trial began on 22 May 1786, in the Palais de Justice on the island in the Seine. It was the sensation of the age, with all Europe agog for the verdict. On 31 May the judges acquitted Cagliostro and Mlle d'Oliva. Villette was exiled for life. The Count and Countess de La Motte were sentenced to flogging, branding, and life imprisonment – he in his absence. The Cardinal, to the public's joy, was acquitted but deprived of his offices and banished from Paris.

Officially it was all over. But for the many people who hated the Queen it provided one more piece of ammunition. Although she was completely innocent in the affair she was held up to ridicule, and the sagging French monarchy was pushed one step nearer disaster. Rohan left France after the Revolution and died in Germany in 1803. Cagliostro was arrested and condemned by the Inquisition for practising Freemasonry, dying in prison. The Count was never caught, and his wife, after her gruesome public branding, escaped from the Salpetrière prison. From London she wrote scandalous, fantasy-filled memoirs bitterly attacking Marie Antoinette. She died after a fall from a window, at the age of thirty-five, not living long enough to see the beheading on 16 October 1793 of her hated enemy, Marie Antoinette.

Rightful
king or shameless
impostor?
Perkin Warbeck, pretender

In 1491, a seventeen-year-old apprentice arrived at Cork in Ireland with his master, a Breton merchant called Pregent Meno who had come to Ireland in the course of his trading business. The boy had been brought up in France. He was handsome, debonair, gay, and wore his clothes with the air of a royal prince. But it was not his good looks that caused the people of Cork to stop in their tracks and gape at him in wonder as he passed. They were astounded by his incredible likeness to the popular King Edward IV of England, who had died some years previously. Surely, they whispered, he must be some relation of Edward's, a prince of royal blood?

There was tremendous excitement in the town as the news of the young man's appearance spread. Who was he, people asked one another? Where had he come from? All sorts of possibilities were raised; but the one that took firmest root in people's minds was that the boy was one of the sons of the dead King Edward IV, one of the two young Princes supposedly murdered in the Tower of London by their uncle, King Richard III. The younger of the two, Richard of York, they argued, must somehow have escaped from the Tower, and had now reappeared in Ireland.

The news soon reached the powerful Irish Earls of

Desmond and Kildare, who were elated at such an opportunity to cause trouble for Henry VII, the King of England, who was trying to curb their power. The two Earls met the boy, and, impressed by his extraordinary resemblance to Edward IV, they persuaded him to say that he was the rightful Duke of York, and that, as such, he should seize 'his' inheritance from the usurper, Henry VII. The boy's name was Perkin Warbeck, and this meeting with the Earls was a momentous one for him. It marked the beginning of his bitter, unrelenting struggle against Henry that was to last for six years.

Henry VII had come to the throne of England by defeating King Richard III at the Battle of Bosworth in 1485. This was the last great battle in the Wars of the Roses, fought between the Houses of Lancaster (the red rose) and York (white). The Wars had torn England apart for over 100 years, and Henry (a Lancastrian) was determined that they should end. Now, however, with the appearance of Perkin Warbeck on the scene, he was confronted with his greatest fear – if this young man were *really* the son of Edward IV (and everyone said that the likeness was extraordinary), then he had a better claim to the throne than Henry himself, who had merely seized the throne by conquest. It seemed to Henry that the Wars of the Roses were about to begin all over again.

The news of the arrival in Ireland of the rightful heir to the English throne soon spread to the rest of Europe. The monarchs of nearly all the European countries were keenly interested. Nothing pleased them more than to see England weakened by internal conflict, and they immediately threw their support behind the mysterious Warbeck. Charles VIII, King of France, who was at war with Henry, invited Perkin to the French court, where he was treated like the Royal Duke he said he was. But when France and England made peace, Henry insisted that Perkin be expelled from France.

Perkin left France for the Netherlands, where Margaret, Dowager Duchess of Burgundy and sister of Edward IV, examined him, and declared that he was the image of her dead brother, and must indeed be the nephew she had thought dead. Her certainty about Perkin convinced the other European monarchs. Maximilian, soon to become Holy Roman Emperor, installed Perkin in state at Antwerp. He was given a guard of twenty archers, all wearing the Yorkist emblem of the white rose as their badge. He displayed the royal arms of England on his house, which infuriated English visitors to the town.

Perkin was proving to be the focus for all Henry's enemies, and was becoming more and more dangerous as his following grew among the powerful monarchs of Europe. So far Henry had treated the matter with contempt, but he could not so lightly dismiss the great invasion of England planned by Perkin and Maximilian in 1495. Perkin arrived off the coast of Deal in Kent on 3 July 1495 with fourteen ships. He had at last come to claim 'his' throne. But the people of Kent would not allow him even to land, and captured the 200 men he had sent ashore as an advance guard. These prisoners were then dragged off to London and Henry, and most of them were hanged.

Perkin's first attempt had ended in disaster. He fled, disappointed, to Ireland where he made contact with the Earl of Desmond. Together they attacked and besieged the town of Waterford, which was still loyal to Henry VII. The siege lasted eleven days, but Perkin's men were forced to withdraw, and his ships were captured. Frustrated in Ireland, he turned to Scotland.

King James IV of Scotland was Henry's greatest enemy. He was always on the lookout for an opportunity to injure Henry in any way. The arrival of Perkin Warbeck provided the ideal excuse. When Perkin came to Scotland in November 1495, he was given a welcome fit for a king. Jousts were even held in his honour. James was impressed by his princely bearing and really seemed to believe that Perkin was the Duke of York. He treated Perkin accordingly, even giving him as his wife the beautiful Lady Catherine Gordon, daughter of the Earl of Huntly, and a cousin of James's.

But Perkin was anxious to get on with his campaign, and he and James began to plan the invasion of England. On 20 September 1496 they marched south. But the invasion was a fiasco. As they marched south, Perkin was thoroughly shocked by the behaviour of James's men in burning towns, killing men, women, and children, and robbing houses. He protested to James about the senseless slaughter of 'his' people, as he called them, but James had lost all patience with him. Why, he replied, take such pains to preserve the realm of another prince? Anyway, Perkin was obviously not wanted in England as no one had rallied to his support, and James realized that he could not go on supporting such a lost cause as Perkin's seemed to be. He was angry at Perkin's interference in the conduct of the Scottish army, and after the retreat back into Scotland, dismissed him from the Court. However, he never stopped believing that Perkin was the real heir to the English throne, and openly sympathized with him right up to the end.

The threat from Scotland had given Henry an excuse to levy more taxes in England, for he was always short of money, but he chose the wrong time to tax the English. The campaign against the Scots to them was just a 'small commotion' and they resented having to pay for what seemed to them to be a minor skirmish, like all the other border raids. Discontent at the new taxes exploded into open revolt in Cornwall under Thomas Flamank, a lawyer, and Michael Joseph, a blacksmith.

Perkin realized that here was his greate chance – a revolt in England itself against Henry. If he could only get his foot inside the door, the rest would be easy. He went to Ireland with his wife, but the Irish, too, were out of sympathy with him – he had been losing for too long, and Henry had been winning. They planned to capture him and hand him over to Henry, but he escaped just in time, and sailed away from Ireland. The Irish ships chased him, forced his ship to heave-to, and boarded it. Perkin's crew was promised a huge reward if they would hand Perkin over, but they refused, and swore that they had never heard of him. The ship was searched, but Perkin was not found, although he was hiding all the time in a pipe in the bows of the ship.

So he came to Cornwall, for what he knew must be his final attempt to seize the throne. If he were to fail this time, there could not be another chance. Leaving his wife at St. Michael's Mount in the very west of Cornwall, he set out for Exeter, joined by about 3,000–4,000 peasants of the county. He had himself proclaimed King Richard IV after landing at White-

The peasant army supporting Perkin Warbeck trudges wearily to Taunton after its defeat at Exeter. Perkin's last, desperate effort had ended in failure.

sand Bay near Land's End. By the time he reached Exeter and laid siege to it, he had 8,000 men, but his peasant army was doomed to failure from the first, because they had no armour and no weapons. The assault was easily repelled by the men of Exeter, 400 of his men being killed and many captured. Weary and exhausted by the struggle, Perkin's peasant band withdrew to Taunton. But the position was now desperate. Cornered by Henry's armies, Perkin fled for his life with sixty of his followers, leaving the peasants, who had so loyally followed him, to their fate.

Pursued by Henry's men, Perkin arrived at Beaulieu where he obtained sanctuary, but he knew there was no way out. The only thing to do was to surrender, and this he did on 5 October 1496, making a full confession of his imposture. He was led through the streets in shame, and was then imprisoned. In June 1498 he escaped, and hid on the banks of the River Thames. He was recaptured and put into a dungeon next to the cell of the Earl of Warwick, a nephew of Edward IV, and the only other Yorkist endangering Henry's safety on the throne.

Henry now thought up a plan to get rid of both his Yorkist rivals at one blow. He introduced one of his secret agents into the Tower, and the agent proceeded to plan the escape of Warwick and Perkin, carrying notes back and forth between them. These notes were shown to the King, and Henry pounced on this certain evidence of treason as his excuse. Perkin and Warwick were tried, and sentenced to death for plotting to escape. They had fallen neatly into the trap. Warwick was beheaded, and Perkin Warbeck was hanged at Tyburn in November 1499. It was the end of a remarkable career, and a short one, for Perkin was only twenty-five when he was executed.

Was Perkin Warbeck really the Duke of York or was he merely an unprincipled adventurer? There is no way of knowing for certain. His likeness to Edward IV was so remarkable that it is possible he may have been his illegitimate son, for Edward spent some time in exile in France, and it is quite feasible that the baby was raised by foster-parents in Tournai, France. Perkin admitted that he was the son of John Osbeck, a merchant of Tournai, but his confession was published abroad after his capture, and could have been Henry's work. He may really have believed that he had a good claim to the throne as the illegitimate heir of Edward IV, and pretended to be Richard of York to make his claim stronger, for he could not have succeeded to the throne if he were illegitimate.

On the other hand Perkin Warbeck may have been a downright impostor. He was certainly a conceited, ambitious young man; and his head was doubtless turned by the flattering attentions of the Irish Earls and the great European princes who made him a tool in their intrigues against Henry.

Whatever Perkin was, one thing is certain. With him and the Yorkist threat safely out of the way, Henry never again had to face a dangerous threat to his throne. The stage was now set for the emergence of the Tudor Golden Age, which was to reach its glorious climax in the reign of Elizabeth I, the grand-daughter of Henry VII.

Murder
in the Cathedral
of Florence
The treachery of the Pazzi

Lorenzo de Medici had many enemies. This was not surprising considering that he and his family had been ruling Florence for over thirty years. For in 15th-century Florence a man made enemies quickly, and those in power made them quicker than most. The Medici family had first assumed control of the Florentine government back in 1434. Now, in 1478, they were one of the most ruthless and powerful families in all Italy. On the other hand they had made Florence into a centre of culture, a byword for pomp and pageantry, and hundreds of artists, poets, and sculptors flocked to seek their patronage.

But not everyone in Florence revelled in the glory of their powerful leaders. Lorenzo, as head of the Medici, was the object of considerable hatred. None of the other families in Florence seemed to have the Medici's knack of manipulating votes and the people who voted; and many were outwardly jealous of the Medici's privileged position. Why should the Florentine Republic, they argued, be run by this particular family and not by another? One family in particular thought along these lines – the Pazzi, who were in fact related to the Medici by marriage. Envious of the Medici's influence, they began to search around for excuses to get rid of them and to take over their power. These excuses were not hard to find and by 1478 their anger had reached boiling-point. Only the deaths of Lorenzo and Giuliano, his brother, would satisfy them.

The date for the assassination of the two Medici brothers was set for Easter Sunday, 26 April 1478. Both Lorenzo and Giuliano would be at Mass that day in the Cathedral, and the conspirators were certain that, under cover of the service, they could strike quickly and successfully. When the deed was done, Jacopo Pazzi, the head of the Pazzi family, was to ride through the streets of Florence with the cry of 'People and Liberty', and raise the city in revolt against the Medici family.

The man chosen as the assassin of Lorenzo, a captain named Montesecco, refused to have any part in the affair if it was to take place during a church service. So the leaders of the conspiracy appointed two priests instead, who had their own grudges against the Medici, and had no qualms about committing murder in a place of worship. Two more men were instructed to deal with Giuliano, and both murders were to be committed at a pre-arranged signal, the ringing of the sanctuary bell.

To the Pazzi family the plan seemed foolproof. At one stroke the two leading members of the family that had controlled the Florentine Republic for over thirty years would be removed, and the Pazzi themselves could take over their power. Moreover, Pope Sixtus IV had expressed his approval of the plan to overthrow the Medici, and although he was not actually in favour of killing Lorenzo, he was far too keen to rid himself of the troublesome Medici to worry unduly about the manner of their disposal. For some years past there had been no love lost between Rome and Florence, particularly as the Medici were the most powerful bankers in Italy, and frequently supplied money to, or withheld it from the Papacy. Sixtus had his eyes on cities and land in and around Florentine territory and he would be glad to see Lorenzo out of the way. It would be much better to have the Pazzi in control of Florence than Lorenzo. 'If he were expelled,' remarked Sixtus, 'we could do as we willed with the Republic.'

Also in on the plot were Girolamo Riario, the nephew of the Pope, who wanted to enlarge his possessions at the expense of Florentine territory – without fear of retaliation from Lorenzo; and Francesco Salviati, whose attempts to be appointed Archbishop of Pisa, a town under Florentine control, had been frustrated for three long years by Lorenzo. Last but by no means least was Francesco Pazzi, manager of the branch of the family bank at Rome. Each conspirator had his own motive for joining the plot, and with such a formidable force arrayed against the Medici, the Pazzi were confident of success.

However, when Easter Sunday came, Lorenzo arrived at the Cathedral without Giuliano. This the conspirators had not allowed for; they had automatically assumed that the two would arrive together and sit together, but Giuliano was not feeling well and had decided to remain at home. Immediately, Francesco Pazzi and an accomplice went out to look for him, and when they found him, persuaded him that he really should attend the service. They offered to accompany him. On the way Francesco put his arm round Giuliano in a gesture of friendship, but really, it is said, to see if the victim was wearing any mail.

Naturally the young man, suspecting nothing, had not bothered to put on any protective clothing.

Towards the end of the Mass, the sanctuary bell sounded, the signal for attack. Knives flashed, and Giuliano reeled against Francesco, who immediately stabbed him in the chest. Then he and other members of the Pazzi family fell upon Giuliano, striking him repeatedly until his body was covered with nineteen wounds. In his maddened frenzy Francesco inflicted a serious wound on his own leg, and as soon as he was sure Giuliano was dead he limped off to his house, bleeding heavily.

Lorenzo, however, had better luck than his unfortunate brother. The two priests assigned to murder him were not as expert in their work, and the first blow missed him completely. The second thrust just grazed his neck as he turned his head away. Wrapping his cloak over his left arm as a shield, Lorenzo drew his sword, and for a while held his adversaries at bay. Then turning, he leapt over the low wooden railing that divided the choir from the nave, and ran in front of the altar to the sacristy, where some friends had already managed to find safety. They just succeeded in slamming the huge bronze doors shut in the faces of the pursuers, and then one of them bent over Lorenzo and sucked the wound in case the dagger which had grazed him had been poisoned.

Few of the spectators had time to realize what was happening, and as the slam of the doors echoed through the Cathedral, pandemonium broke out. Some people thought the roof had caved in. Many fled to their homes, while others rushed to take up arms in defence of Lorenzo. Soon all Florence knew of the attempt on the lives of the Medici brothers, and

To celebrate the failure of the conspiracy, Lorenzo de Medici had this medal struck. One side bears his own head (top), the other shows Giuliano, his murdered brother.

when Jacopo Pazzi rode through the streets crying 'People and Liberty', he was met with curses and jeers, and cries of support for the Medici. At that point he must have known that the conspiracy on which his family had staked so much was a failure. They had completely misinterpreted the popular feeling towards the Medici, and now, with Lorenzo still alive, there would be no hope at all of gaining power.

The Archbishop of Pisa, with a handful of supporters, had left the Cathedral before the attack, and gone to take possession of the palace where the elected members of the government were gathered. Leaving his men outside the chamber, the Archbishop went in to the magistrates on the pretext of having something to communicate on the Pope's behalf. But the chief magistrate, Cesare Petrucci, suspected that something was wrong. The Archbishop stuttered with fright and kept glancing round to see if the reinforcements he expected had arrived. He did not know, of course, that the conspiracy had already misfired and that no help would come. Petrucci sensed his unease and called out for the guards to drag a chain across the stairs to prevent the intruders from leaving. From the commotion in the streets, he guessed that an attack had been made on the Medici, and news confirming his suspicions soon reached him, and probably decided him on action. He waited until the people had gathered in the square below, then hung from the windows of the palace the Archbishop, together with Francesco Pazzi, who had been hauled from the bed in which he was nursing his gashed leg.

A rumour spread that Lorenzo had been killed as well, and the people were delighted when he showed himself at the window of his house, his neck swathed in bandages. They demanded that he take revenge on the traitors, who had so brutally murdered Giuliano, one of the best-loved men in Florentine society. Lorenzo was not slow in doing their bidding. Indeed, so bloody was the retribution that one man later said, 'it passed all civilized bounds'. Nearly a hundred people were killed, many of them completely innocent. The two priests who had attacked Lorenzo were discovered in hiding a few days later and brought back to Florence. Before being hanged, their ears and noses were sliced off. Montesecco was given a soldier's death by the sword, and Jacopo Pazzi was tortured and hanged. Few, indeed, of the Pazzi family escaped the wrath of the Florentines. Those who did suffered lasting shame and humiliation.

The Pazzi conspiracy was a fiasco. And the scores of corpses swaying gently from the windows of that Florentine palace were a grisly reminder of what lay in store for future conspirators if they, too, were unsuccessful.

The English seaman who became a Japanese noble

The strange story of William Adams

Barely moments after the anchor dropped, dozens of nimble little men swarmed over the side of the ship. Totally ignoring the occupants they instantly set about carrying off the cargo and any other items of value they could lay their hands on. While their ship was being openly looted by these Japanese intruders the officers and crew made no attempt to defend their possessions. In fact they scarcely paid any attention at all. Instead, they lay sprawled out on the deck, listless, starving, more dead than alive. All but twenty-four of the crew of 110 had perished, and of the survivors no more than seven were able to stand upright.

The date was 19 April 1600, and one of these exhausted mariners, William Adams, was the first Englishman ever to set eyes on Japan. It was an ominous beginning.

Twenty-two months earlier five ships had confidently set out from Rotterdam bound for the Far East. William Adams had leapt at the offer to join the expedition as pilot on one of the ships, *Liefde* (Charity). He was thirty-four years old, and after a boyhood apprenticeship to a ship builder in Limehouse, Kent, he had spent almost all his time at sea, in the service of both English and Dutch merchants. And when the chance came to pilot a ship to the other side of the world he was not the sort of man to turn it down.

It had been a terrible journey, southwards across the Atlantic, through the Magellan Straits at the tip of South America, and across the Pacific. The five ships were flung apart by storms after leaving the Straits of Magellan; one turned back to Holland, another sailed on to the East Indies and was captured by the Portuguese, another fell prey to the Spaniards, and a fourth sank. Only *Liefde* managed to reach the destination, Japan.

But the long, storm-wracked journey had exacted a terrible toll. Food ran low, the crew grew weaker, and starvation set in. If *Liefde* had not staggered into the coastal waters of Japan when she did there would have been no survivors at all.

As it was, the few men remaining were in very serious trouble. They were in a country about which they knew practically nothing, among people who were absolutely foreign to them. Fortunately, the inhabitants of Oita, on the north-east coast of the Japanese island of Kyushu, were content to plunder the stricken ship. Before anything worse could happen the local lord arrived on the scene, ordered *Liefde* brought into harbour, and the men taken ashore. There they were fed, housed, and treated with every courtesy, while the lord sent word of their arrival to the most powerful noble in Japan, a man named Ieyasu.

Ieyasu was in the middle of waging a civil war that would soon make him Shogun, or ruler of Japan. He was a clever, far-sighted man, and the news brought to him about a strange ship from the other side of the world excited his interest. He immediately ordered that one of the foreigners be brought to him. The man chosen was William Adams.

Ieyasu was not the only person interested in the arrival of a Dutch ship in Japanese waters. Word also reached the ears of Jesuit missionaries from Portugal, who half a century earlier, had managed to gain a foothold in Japan. Although the Japanese strongly disapproved of the Portuguese attempts at converting people to Christianity, they had tolerated the situation because they were very keen to develop trade with Europe.

These Portuguese missionaries were extremely alarmed at this intrusion by Dutch mariners. If the Dutch were to begin trading with Japan, then Portugal would be faced with stiff competition. Even worse, the Dutch were Protestants, and this was an era of bitter religious hatred. These Dutchmen would surely interfere with the important task of converting the Japanese to the Roman Catholic faith.

The Portuguese missionaries promptly informed Ieyasu that the Dutch were pirates, fierce war-makers who could only bring Japan trouble. In their opinion, Ieyasu would be wise to put them to death immediately.

The Portuguese warning disturbed Ieyasu greatly, but, fortunately for Adams and the Dutchmen, he refused to be rushed. He was determined to give the newcomers a hearing, but of course if he decided the Portuguese were right he would not hesitate to have them killed.

So, when Will Adams left his Dutch comrades and set out for the town of Osaka, where Ieyasu was

William Adams is interviewed by Ieyasu. He explains, with the aid of charts, where England is, and how he and his Dutch shipmates had managed to reach Japan.

awaiting him, he carried the fate of the entire expedition in his hands. On 12 May 1600 he made his appearance before the all-powerful Ieyasu.

In answer to Ieyasu's probing questions Adams explained that he was an Englishman, and tried to describe where England was on the map. He explained further that the English (and of course the Dutch) wished to begin trading with Japan, and that such a trade would be profitable for both parties. When Ieyasu asked whether or not the English were a warlike people – after all he had known the Jesuits for a long time and they might well be telling the truth – Adams stoutly denied the charge. The only people the English were at war with, he said, were the Portuguese and Spanish. The Dutch sided with the English in this struggle, and with all other nations they were at peace.

This reply made sense to Ieyasu, since it explained why the Portuguese Jesuits were so keen to have these strangers killed. But he still wanted to think it over, so he dismissed Adams from his presence and ordered him to be locked up in jail. Adams recorded later that he was very worried by this turn of events and lived in daily fear of being put to death. He was even more alarmed to discover that the Japanese method of execution was crucifixion.

Twice more over the next six weeks Ieyasu had Adams brought before him for questioning, and each time he became more and more convinced that the plain-spoken Englishman was telling the truth. On the third occasion he decided that he liked Adams very much indeed, released him, and sent him to join his shipmates – who were now also in Osaka, where Liefde had been brought on Ieyasu's instructions.

The Dutch were overjoyed by Adams' return. They had received no news over the long weeks and feared the worst. Six of them had died from the after-effects of the voyage, and those who remained fully expected every minute to be their last. And the prospect of crucifixion sent shivers up and down the bravest spine.

Despite Adams' triumphant return, however, uncertainty still remained. If the Japanese were not going to kill them, were they free to sail for home? Apparently not. After a month of idleness, during which time 50,000 Spanish dollars that had been plundered were returned on Ieyasu's orders, they were told to sail to Tokyo, where Ieyasu normally lived.

In Tokyo things continued much the same. The months dragged by and most of the 50,000 dollars was wasted in bribing court officials – unsuccessfully – to secure their release. Ieyasu had no intention of allowing them to return to Europe. Finally, when the money was almost all gone, what little remained was divided among the mariners and they went their separate ways, free to shift for themselves but exiled forever from their homes. To ease their lot, however, Ieyasu granted each man a small annual pension, and two pounds of rice a day.

Throughout this entire period Will Adams had been rising higher and higher in Ieyasu's estimation. The Shogun (as Ieyasu now styled himself) spent many long hours in conversation with Adams, eagerly picking his brain for European learning of all sorts. In particular, Ieyasu developed a keen interest in mathematics, and Adams gained great favour by acting as his tutor. He even managed to summon his ship-building knowledge from boyhood and supervised the construction of two European ships. Ieyasu was delighted, and lavish with his rewards. He made Adams a Japanese noble, and gave him a large country estate complete with almost a hundred retainers.

So it was that William Adams, a few short years after his brush with death, became a high-ranking Japanese noble, an adviser and close friend to the Shogun, and a wealthy landowner to boot. The only request his friend Ieyasu refused to grant him was the liberty to return to England, and so, finally convinced that he would never see his home again, Will Adams took the last step in his transformation from English mariner to Japanese noble. He married a Japanese woman, who bore him two children, a boy Joseph and a girl, Susanna.

But Will Adams was not content to live out the rest of his life in the ease and luxury of his new position. He was a restless, energetic man and he threw himself into the quickly-expanding business of trade. Because of his unique position as friend and adviser to the Shogun his services were much in demand by his old friends the Dutch, and even by his old enemies the Portuguese. Having failed miserably in their attempts to secure his death, or prevent his rise to great influence, the Portuguese were sensible enough to admit defeat and try to win his friendship.

Adams was quite willing to do business with his old enemies, but of course he never forgot how nearly they had been the cause of his death. And even when the Spaniards appeared a few years later – and the Spaniards were even greater enemies of the English than were the Portuguese – Adams provided them with much valuable help in their efforts to open up trade with his adopted country.

Trouble began, however, when English merchants first arrived on the scene. The British East India company had become interested in the idea of trade with Japan chiefly because they had heard, from Dutch sources, that some unknown Englishman named William Adams enjoyed immense influence with the ruler. Adams had encouraged this interest in occasional letters written to the East India Company, and when the commander of a British trading fleet, Captain John Saris, turned up in June 1613, he naturally had high hopes that this man Adams would secure special advantages for his fellow-countrymen.

Adams and Saris took an immediate dislike to each other. Saris was arrogant and contemptuous of Adams' Japanese friends. He wrote in his diary that Adams behaved like a 'naturalized Jappaner'. Even worse, although Adams seemed pleased to help the English join in the growing trade with Japan, he seemed equally happy to offer his services not only to the Dutch, who were rapidly becoming bitter rivals of the English, but also the Portuguese and Spanish, enemies of long standing. This man wasn't a very patriotic Englishman!

The truth was that Adams *was* very much a 'naturalized Jappaner'. He had adopted his new home completely, and when, at length, his friend the Shogun offered to let him return to England, he decided against it. To Adams, quarrels between the various countries of distant Europe had little to do with him, and although he was finally persuaded by Saris to work for the East India Company, he resigned after three years, preferring to devote his time to his own business interests.

By the time of his death, in 1620, relations between

the various European traders and their Japanese hosts had deteriorated greatly, mainly because very few of the Europeans had Adams' knack for adjusting to so different a civilization. Within the next twenty years almost all were ordered to leave, and two centuries would pass before Japan was once again open to the West.

But the Japanese never forgot their old friend Will Adams. Today, in Tokyo, there is a street called 'Anjin Cho' (Pilot Street), named in his honour, and a memorial stone set in a prominent place. Each day people of the district arrange flowers around his memorial stone and then place a glass of water near it so that the spirit of Will Adams can drink.

The man they called 'the Scourge of God'

Attila the Hun

In the year A.D. 376, officers commanding the garrison on the River Danube, the north-eastern frontier of the Roman Empire, began hearing alarming reports of turmoil amongst the barbarians who lived to the north. Rumour swept the Empire that an unknown race of unbelievable savagery had poured into the area, burning, looting, killing, and driving the inhabitants on before them. As nation fell back upon nation in a desperate attempt to flee the invader, shock waves were felt all the way to the Danube.

But it was hoped that the reports were very exaggerated, as such things normally are. Suddenly, however, swarms of terrified people began appearing on the other side of the Danube, pleading to be let into the Empire. Day after day thousands of panic-stricken barbarians, who had always kept proudly aloof from the Empire, streamed inside, begging for safety.

The Romans now knew that something was seriously wrong. The Emperor and his advisers, in Constantinople, were alarmed. Who, they asked, were these terrifying savages from the very ends of the earth, who had so suddenly, and without warning, hurled themselves upon Europe? They were soon to find out.

They were about to witness the first appearance of the Hun, a name that would come to strike terror into the hearts of the bravest men; a race that would throw up a leader who would come within a razor's edge of destroying the entire civilized world: Attila the Hun, the man they called 'the Scourge of God'.

The mighty Roman Empire, at the time of the Huns' appearance, had been in decline for many years. In fact, for all practical purposes, it was no longer a united empire at all. There was an emperor of the East, in Constantinople, and an emperor of the West, in Rome. The pomp and grandeur of the Empire lingered on, but the real power was gradually being sapped. Both in the east and the west, the Romans were surrounded by nations of barbarians, hostile to the Empire, but fortunately for the Romans, equally hostile to one another. By shrewdly playing one nation off against the other, the Romans had managed, but only just, to keep from being submerged by the barbarians. It was a dangerous game the Romans played, but there was nothing else they could do, when their enemies, taken together, were powerful enough to sweep them from the face of the earth. The two empires existed in a perilous state, now at war with one group of barbarians, now with another, often with the enemy in the last war an ally in the next.

The big question was, could they fit the savage Huns into this complicated, deadly serious game? It appeared they could. For the next fifty years or so, although from time to time they made devastating raids into Roman territory, these Huns were uneasy allies about as often as they were frightening enemies.

A little gold, and a lot of flattery, managed to keep them in check.

But trouble was brewing. In the year 434, the ruler of the Huns, Rua, was enraged to discover that the Romans were secretly giving aid to other tribes who were deadly enemies of the Huns. Furthermore, the Romans were not sending back the Huns who, for one reason or another, deserted and went to live inside the Empire. This could mean war, and Rua sent a few of his men to Constantinople to protest, and, if necessary, to threaten. Certain that they could soothe the Hun's ruffled feathers, the Emperor Theodosius sent envoys back to Rua to talk things over.

But by the time they arrived at the frontier of the Empire, near the Danube, a most unfortunate thing had happened; unfortunate for the Romans, that is. Rua was dead. The Roman envoys were led into the presence of his successor, his nephew Attila.

They saw a fur-clad man in his mid-thirties, short but very strongly built. His skin was sallow, his head was massive, and his nose was broad and flat. He regarded them impassively with dark, very deeply-set eyes. He did not dismount from his horse, nor did he invite his guests to, which was most uncomfortable for the Romans. They were not in the habit of conducting diplomacy from horseback, but this man Attila did not look the sort one would wish to quarrel with.

Even worse than this discourtesy, the insolent barbarian did not appear the slightest bit interested in negotiating anything. He simply stated his terms. The Romans must instantly and permanently stop supporting the enemies of the Huns. They must immediately send back all Hun fugitives and escaped

Roman prisoners – or pay a heavy ransom for them! Finally, they must double the 350 pounds of gold they paid in tribute to the Huns each year. Attila would have his own way or he would have a war. He had his way.

The envoys returned to Constantinople painfully aware that this man Attila meant the Roman Empire no good. Something would have to be done.

For the time being, however, he gave them no more trouble. He had more important things to do than engage in petty disputes with Roman envoys. For the next five years Attila travelled the length and breadth of the Hunnish Empire, which stretched from the Caspian Sea in the east almost to the Rhine in the west. He had inherited a loosely-joined host of completely uncivilized tribes, a people suffering from grinding poverty who had wandered slowly west from the great wastes of central Asia, driving their flocks before them. It was Attila's dream to forge these tribes into the most terrifying military machine known to mankind. Tirelessly, he moved amongst his people, rallying them to his cause, banding the tribes together into one great united force. Cavalry was his weapon, and the Hunnish cavalry was probably the finest the world has ever seen. The entire race practically lived on horseback, and Attila's mounted warriors could shower an enemy with arrows with unbelievable speed and accuracy. Ready to strike at last, Attila cunningly bided his time, waiting for the right moment.

And strike he did! In 441 the Huns descended upon the Eastern Empire with a vengeance. On one pretext or another the lightning cavalry of Attila devastated the Roman fortifications along the Danube, and then turned south into the heartland of the Empire. Over the next three years the Romans struggled helplessly as the marauding Huns roamed at will looting, burning, killing. The Roman soldiers were terrified by the very sight of them. Men said of the Huns that the grass never grew again when they had passed over it. Finally, realizing the hopelessness of trying to drive the Huns out by force, the Emperor Theodosius sued for peace.

As usual, it cost the Empire dearly. The price of ransoming Roman prisoners went up, and the tribute (blackmail really) of 700 pounds of gold was to be trebled. Nor did the Romans buy peace for long. Representatives of Attila continually turned up in Constantinople, demanding further concessions. Even if they did not always get what they asked for, they always received handsome gifts – a Roman tradition. Probably, the main reason for sending envoy after envoy was just to increase the wealth of the Huns in this painless way.

With the Eastern Empire virtually eating out of his hand, Attila turned his attentions to the West. He knew he could finish Constantinople off any time he pleased, but it would be a good thing to bring Rome to heel first.

All he needed was an excuse, and as if by magic, one appeared. The sister of the Emperor Valentinian, the Emperor of the West, was a woman named Honoria. Completely out of the blue she sent one of her servants to Attila, with the astonishing proposal that she become Attila's wife. Before Attila could reply, the scheme reached the ears of Valentinian, who promptly banished Honoria from the Court, and informed Attila that she was mad. Attila, he hoped, had not

A Roman coin bearing the head of Theodosius II, the Emperor of the East during the time of Attila. Again and again his Empire was overrun and held to ransom by the 'Scourge of God'.

A Roman coin bearing the head of Valentinian III, the Emperor of the West during the time of Attila. Attila claimed the Emperor's sister as his wife and half the Empire as her dowry.

taken the marriage proposal seriously. Attila replied that he did indeed take the proposal seriously, and that he claimed Honoria for his wife with half the Western Empire as her dowry. Valentinian, of course, refused even to consider such a thing. Attila determined to take it by force. He would settle the Roman Empire once and for all.

In case Valentinian should be in any doubt as to his intentions, Attila sent an ambassador to the Emperor, with the supremely arrogant command that the Imperial palace be made ready for *his* arrival.

This brutal message was not lost on the Romans. Suddenly aware of the terrible danger to their Empire, they wasted no more time and energy in exchanging messages with the Hun. Envoys scurried throughout the length and breadth of the Empire, pleading with .the various nations of barbarians to bury their differences, and make common cause against the Hun. In particular, the great Roman general, Aetius, moved heaven and earth to patch up a twenty-year-old quarrel with Theodoric, the powerful King of the Visigoths, or West Goths. It was absolutely essential, Aetius made clear, for the survival of the Visigoths as well as the Romans that they stand united against the savage hordes of Attila. It was, without exaggeration, a matter of life or death. Theodoric, knowing full well that the Huns were about to descend upon his kingdom like a pack of wolves, could scarcely disagree. The alliance was made – in the nick of time.

Early in the year 450, the armies of Attila flung themselves upon the West. Sweeping across the Rhine, the barbaric hordes carried all before them. As Aetius raced north to join Theodoric city after city fell before the Hun.

Finally, on a plain not far from Orléans, in what is now northern France, the combined armies of Aetius and Theodoric came face to face with the horsemen of Attila. All day the battle raged furiously. Both sides suffered terrible casualties – Theodoric himself was slain – but at nightfall the Huns were driven back. They had been defeated in one of the most crucial battles ever fought. Had they won, the entire Western world would have lain at their feet.

As it was, Attila and his men straggled back to their homes beyond the Danube, and after one brief raid the next year they never again threatened the West.

But the East was no longer to be spared. If he could not take Rome Attila was certain he could take Constantinople. Marcian, the new Emperor (Theodoric had died), must have shuddered as the news filtered in that the entire Hun army was getting ready to move in his direction.

But the mighty Hun would trouble Europe no more. On the very eve of the invasion, Attila, following the custom of his race, took another wife to add to the many he already had. The girl, beautiful and young, was named Ildico. Attila was now in his fifties, but he drank and caroused during the wedding celebrations like a man half his age. Exhausted at last, he staggered off to bed. He fell asleep on his back, and while unconscious, he suffered a terrible nose bleed. Because he was lying on his back, the blood poured down his throat and drowned him.

That very night the Emperor Marcian, far away in Constantinople, awoke with a start from a frighteningly vivid dream. In this dream, he had seen a bow snapped in half. He hurriedly assembled his wise men and soothsayers. What, he demanded, did the dream foretell? He was told that the dream meant a deadly enemy had perished.

Late the following morning, Attila's friends and attendants became concerned about his absence and went to his room. The door was locked and there was no answer to their shouts. Panic-stricken, they broke down the door and found Attila dead, and Ildico lying in the corner weeping. In their despair and grief, the men cut off part of their hair and slashed their faces horribly with their swords, so that their king might be mourned not with woman's tears but by manly blood.

Attila's body was laid out in a silk tent in the middle of a plain, and the very finest horsemen rode round and round the tent in honour of their dead king. Then a crowd of people gathered and sang a great song describing all Attila's victories. At last, they placed his body in a barrow and covered him with gold and silver and iron; iron because with his mighty sword he had conquered nations, gold and silver because he had forced tribute from the proud Roman Empire. On top of it all they laid the weapons of his defeated enemies. Then, in the dead of night, the great casket was buried in a secret place, and so that it remained secret, those who buried him were slaughtered.

The people of the Roman Empire heaved a sigh of relief. They were finally rid of their most deadly foe. Without Attila, they knew they would never have to fear the savage Huns again. They were right. The restless Huns melted away into the forests beyond the Danube, disappearing from the world stage as mysteriously and as quickly as they had arrived.

Above – the medal struck by the Pope, Gregory XIII, to celebrate the Massacre: one side shows his own head and the other an avenging angel. Below – Catherine de Medici gazes out of the window as the Massacre of St. Bartholomew draws to a close. Much of the blame for this appalling deed must lie with her. But her son Charles IX, with his head in his hands, was also responsible. Many Catholics all over France congratulated Charles for allowing the massacre to take place, but by then he was beginning to feel remorse for his part in the affair.

When 20,000 died to please a lady
Catherine de Medici and the Massacre of St. Bartholomew

Admiral Coligny, one of the most important members of the French Protestant religion, or Huguenots as they were called, was walking down a street in Paris on his way to his lodging. It was August 1572. Paris was thronged with Huguenots of noble birth, who had come to celebrate the marriage of their leader, Henry of Navarre, to Margaret, the daughter of the Queen Mother, Catherine de Medici. The event had been marked by three days of festivities: dancing, jousting, and charades. Although there was no love lost between Catholics and Huguenots, it seemed that both parties had put their differences aside for the moment, and willingly joined in the celebrations.

As he went on his way home, Coligny could not have seriously imagined that anyone would make an attempt on his life. Although he had received several warnings not to attend the wedding, he was a trusted adviser and close friend of the King, Charles IX, which was surely a guarantee of his safety. But as he bent down to adjust a shoe, a shot rang out from high up in a nearby house. The bullet missed his heart, but it shattered a finger and passed through his elbow. His attendants stormed the house from which the shot had come, but by then the assailant had escaped.

When news reached the King of this attempt on his friend's life he was furious. He swore to bring the assassin to justice and to find out who was behind the plot. The Huguenots themselves were in no doubt as to who was responsible: it was the Guise family, the leading Catholics in France. But as well as these accusations, which were well founded as it happened, a much more serious and insistent rumour began to spread – that the evil spirit behind the affair was none other than the Queen Mother herself, Catherine de Medici.

Catherine de Medici was at this time fifty-three years of age. Descended from the famous Florentine family, the Medici, she had married into the French royal family in 1533. She was a wily unscrupulous and ambitious woman, and she had a passionate, almost fanatical pride in her children. Indeed, she watched over them so jealously that she even placed her bed in her son Charles' bedroom when he became King in 1560. Living always in his mother's shadow, the unfortunate Charles grew up to be a confused, almost feeble-minded young man.

Catherine fulfilled almost all the duties of king, and when it came to running French affairs she always tried to find a policy that suited the particular occasion. Her main aim was to try to patch up the religious quarrels in France and her first instinct was to be friendly towards the Huguenots. This policy did not please many Catholics and in the end it was to backfire on her. For while she was trying to patch up these quarrels, Admiral Coligny, the Huguenot leader, was rapidly gaining influence over the King.

He kept telling the young Charles that French forces should be sent into the Netherlands to help the people there who were rebelling against their Spanish overlords. Catherine thought this was a foolish idea because Spain, who controlled the Netherlands, would use the excuse of French interference in her affairs to launch a war against France. And this was the last thing Catherine wanted.

But Charles seemed on the point of agreeing with his Huguenot friends, and this was more than Catherine could bear. If he did send troops to help the Dutch rebels, it would be the first time Charles had escaped from his mother's power and gone against her wishes. So, to prevent Charles from making a terrible mistake in French foreign policy, and also to recapture her own influence over him, Catherine began to scheme for the downfall of Coligny.

When she heard that the attempt on Coligny's life had failed, she knew that there was only one thing to do. She went to Charles and confronted him with the news that the Huguenots were up in arms to avenge the attempt, and that the Catholics, tired of Charles' preference for the Huguenots, were preparing to take matters into their own hands. Playing on his fears of civil war, and of assassination attempts on his own person, she told him that nothing short of total elimination of the Huguenots would save France. Charles cowered before his mother's demands and put up no resistance. He agreed, feebly, that the Huguenots must die.

Charles' change of mind is one of the most momentous events in French history. In his confused and unbalanced mind he was quite prepared to believe his mother if she said that his friends one day might be his enemies the next. So from now on he was committed to exterminating the Huguenots, and he agreed to

A contemporary painting of the Massacre of St. Bartholomew, 24 August 1572. The painter, Francois Dubois, is supposed to have been present during the three days' terrible slaughter of the Huguenots. He has included Catherine de Medici in the painting – she stands in the background, in front of the castle, surveying the results of her handiwork.

Catherine's plans for the slaughter of the Huguenots on St. Bartholomew's Day, 24 August 1572.

Plans for the massacre went ahead without a hitch and in the small hours of Sunday, 24 August, the bells sounded for the signal to attack. Anyone not wearing a white handkerchief round their left arm – a sign that they were on the Catholic side – was to be killed immediately. The first to die was Coligny himself. A party of soldiers burst into his house, raced to his room, and struck him down as he knelt in prayer by his bed. His body was thrown down into the street to land at the feet of the Duke of Guise. For the rest of the night Paris was in an uproar. Huguenots were killed in their beds, in the streets, in churches, as they escaped in boats or across rooftops.

Nor did the massacre end when dawn broke. By then, hundreds of bodies littered the centre of Paris, but the slaughter continued for another three days before sanity returned to the Catholics and to Charles IX. It was with some justice that one man later wrote that 'everywhere we have seen rivers of blood and mountains of corpses'. Even Henry of Navarre's attendants were killed, although Charles spared Henry's own life. In the provinces, the slaughter continued, although on a lesser scale. Men used the opportunity afforded by the massacre to pay off old scores, debtors against creditors, Catholics against Huguenots.

Of the various estimates that have been made as to the numbers that died in the massacre, the most likely one is somewhere between 20,000 and 30,000. Protestant countries in Europe were horrified at the affair. Spain, however was delighted that what looked like a very dangerous enemy had been removed from the scene. The Papacy even had a medal struck to celebrate the event. Catholics all over France congratulated Charles on showing such wisdom – but by then the King was filled with remorse at his part in the Massacre.

In fact the Massacre was not as successful as it looked. If Catherine had hoped to eliminate *all* the Huguenots, those hopes were not realized. The main body of Huguenots was much stronger than she imagined and retreated into their fortified cities in the south of France; they lived to fight another day. And the greatest irony of all was the fact that in 1594, Henry of Navarre, the Huguenot prince, became King of France.

'Fight like Englishmen - or die like dogs'
The bloody exploits of Henry Morgan, buccaneer

The city of Panama gleamed in the early morning sun. It was the capital and richest city of the Spanish dominions in central America. Inhabited by wealthy Spaniards, Panama's white stone buildings and handsome wooden houses were full of treasure and merchandise, choice wines and good food.

But on this bright January morning in 1671 the prosperous city on the shore of the Pacific Ocean was threatened by a dark cloud of humanity – the terrifying buccaneer army led by the ruthless Henry Morgan.

Drawn up on the savanna (plain) in front of the city stood 1,200 savage buccaneers, armed to the teeth; they were all bearded, filthy, starving, thirsting for drink, food, and blood. For nine nightmare days they had trekked across the jungle-covered Isthmus of Panama. And now, after the arduous march, the great prize glittered invitingly before their greedy eyes. But the prize was not for easy taking. A Spanish army of some 3,000 soldiers – supported by 2,000 wild bulls – stood between the eager buccaneers and the city.

Suddenly the Spanish cavalry, 600 strong, were charging over the savanna towards Morgan's ragged army, and even the battle-hardened buccaneers must have shivered with fear as the enemy horsemen galloped at them, their razor sharp Toledo blades flashing and waving in the sunshine. But then the rough, steady voice of Henry Morgan filled the air:

'It's too late to tremble now, lads. We have no choice but to fight resolutely or die. We have committed too many cruelties against yonder enemy to expect fair quarter. Fight, then, like Englishmen – or die like dogs!'

Such courage was typical of Morgan. No one ever denied his bravery. Nor could anyone seriously deny that he was grasping, brutal, and treacherous. He must have been the last man on earth the Spanish looked forward to seeing on the outskirts of Panama.

Henry Morgan was born in Wales about 1635. He grew into a big, sturdy, and restless boy who ran away to sea while still a youngster. He sailed to the West Indies, and in Jamaica, the base of pirates and buccaneers, he matured into manhood and became master of a privateer. A privateer captain was one who had a commission, or licence, to attack the ships of any enemy nation at war with his own country. Jamaica was an English colony, and in Morgan's time England was at war with Spain.

The New World was rich in gold, silver, and precious gems, and Spanish ships laden with treasure sailed regularly from the Americas to Spain, and it was these treasure ships that became the main target of pirates and privateers.

Henry Morgan was the most successful privateer of the Caribbean Sea. He had all the necessary qualities. An outstanding leader of men, he was intelligent, cunning, tough, cool-headed in emergencies, greedy for plunder, and merciless to his victims. His name became a word of terror and hatred among the Spanish people in the Americas.

The crews of his ships were mostly recruited from the buccaneers of the West Indies: pirates, naval deserters, ex-slaves, escaped convicts, and villians of every description. The name 'buccaneer', by which all sea robbers came to be known, originated when sailors of various nations decided to give up seafaring and settle on the islands of the Caribbean, where they lived the life of hunters, killing the plentiful wild cattle and selling the meat to ships that called at the islands.

These hunters cured the meat in the native Indian style called 'bukan', in which the meat was cut into strips, laid on a hurdle of green wood and dried over a low fire fed with the fat and bones of the slaughtered animals. And from 'bukan' came 'buccaneer' – a curer of meat. Over the years these buccaneers became a wild and lawless breed, the ideal recruits for pirate and privateer vessels.

Among Henry Morgan's many exploits against the Spaniards three are outstanding: the attack on the fortified town of Porto Bello, on the Isthmus of Panama; the battle of Maracaibo; and the expedition against the city of Panama.

The attack on Porto Bello was a very daring project. Morgan was granted the commission by Sir Thomas Modyford, the Governor of Jamaica (with whom Morgan had a close working relationship), and set sail with twelve small ships and about 700 English and French buccaneers. They landed on the coast some twenty miles from Porto Bello and marched quietly on the town to make a surprise attack.

They silenced the sentries at the first fort that protected the town and surrounded the strongpoint.

Morgan called upon the Spanish garrison to surrender, but the answer was gunfire, which alerted the people of Porto Bello. After a fierce fight the buccaneers captured the fort, and, furious with the soldiers for resisting and thus giving the alarm, they exacted a brutal vengeance. They locked their prisoners in the gunpowder magazine and blew them up.

Morgan and his men then marched on the town. Here they met stiff opposition and were repulsed when they tried to storm the walls. As the buccaneers licked their wounds Morgan had a fiendish idea. He

Henry Morgan, the Welsh-born terror of the Spanish Main.
Right – a 17th-century piece of eight, or Spanish dollar. These gold coins were the buccaneers' most prized booty.

had his men construct a number of wooden ladders, broad enough to allow three or four men to ascend together. He then dragooned a large group of nuns and monks from a nearby convent to carry the scaling ladders to the walls.

Morgan then warned the governor of Porto Bello that if he did not surrender the town he would force the nuns and monks to climb the ladders and act as living shields for his men to follow. But the governor fearful of the terrible fate that would befall the town and its inhabitants if he surrendered to the cut-throat buccaneers, refused to agree to Morgan's demand. And so the heartless invaders compelled the nuns and monks at sword point to climb the ladders of death.

The Spaniards, full of remorse for what they were doing, were forced to fire muskets and throw missiles at their innocent victims, killing and wounding many of them. Then, when the defenders were reloading their guns, the buccaneers swarmed over the walls with yells and howls of triumph. At hand-to-hand fighting they knew no equal; sword, pistol, knife, fist and teeth were used with all the ferocity of a wildcat. After a short but spirited defence the Spaniards were beaten and those that survived the onslaught begged for quarter, all except the governor, who fought on single-handed until he fell under a dozen cutlass blades.

Now that Porto Bello was theirs, the buccaneers went on their usual rampage, looting and killing at will. Prisoners were horribly tortured to make them reveal where they had hidden treasure and other valuables. Morgan returned to Jamaica with considerable plunder and his reputation as a bold and successful privateer rose even higher.

Morgan's next target was the town of Gibraltar,

which lay on the shore of the great lagoon of Maracaibo, on the coast of Venezuala. On this expedition, in
April 1669, Morgan had a dozen little ships and 1,000
men under his command. He shattered with cannon
fire the Castle of Maracaibo, which protected the
narrow mouth of the lagoon, and sailed in to find
Gibraltar vitually deserted. The inhabitants had fled
at his coming, and what riches they could not carry
with them they had hidden.

An angry Morgan sacked the town and spent
several weeks searching for the hidden wealth. He
hunted down inhabitants and tortured them into
telling where the riches were, and in this way amas-
sed a fair amount of booty. But he stayed in the town
too long. For one morning he discovered that he had
been trapped. The Spaniards had repaired the castle
and three large and powerfully armed men-of-war
now blocked the narrow mouth of the lagoon, the
only exit.

But the crafty Morgan was equal to the situation.
He decided to blast his way out by using an explosive
fire-ship. He crammed one of his vessels with tar, pitch,
brimstone, dry leaves, and barrels of gunpowder. To
fool the enemy into thinking the ship was manned, he
lined the decks with dummy figures – logs dressed with
the clothes of his buccaneers and armed with muskets
and swords. Then Morgan set sail for the mouth of the
lagoon with his fleet headed by the fire ship with its
phantom crew, and a slow-burning match in the hold.

On this occasion the Spaniards played right into
Morgan's hands. They were determined on close-
quarter combat, and as the fire-ship came out of the
narrow channel into the sea, the biggest man-of-war

sailed in close and grappling hooks were flung on to the floating bomb. When the dummy buccaneers did not move the Spanish captain realized that he had been fooled, and recognised the fire-ship for what it was. He screamed to his men to release the deadly vessel. But it was too late.

Flames were soon raging. Unable to free their ship from the blazing decoy, the Spanish crew leapt overboard. Then the gunpowder on the fire-ship exploded, sinking the big man-of-war. This violent turn of events shook the confidence of the other Spanish ships and, after a running battle, Morgan and his fleet escaped and returned to Jamaica.

For a while Morgan, who had acquired a large estate in Jamaica, withdrew from privateering and lived peacefully and handsomely on his ill-gotten gains. Then came news that the Spaniards intended to invade Jamaica and rid the Caribbean once and for all of this buccaneer stronghold. To save the island, Governor Modyford made Morgan 'Admiral and Commander-in-Chief of all ships of war belonging to this harbour', with the commission to 'attain, seize and destroy all enemy vessels that come within his reach . . . and to land in the enemy's territory as many men as he shall think needful'.

But barely a week after Morgan had sailed with some thirty ships and about 2,000 men, a peace treaty was signed between England and Spain. It is said that Morgan was notified of the treaty but that he chose to ignore it. For he had already decided to carry out what he called his 'last great venture against the Spaniards', the attack on the city of Panama.

After several successful forays against Spanish shipping, Morgan landed on the central American mainland and took the fortified town of Chagres, in order to open the way to Panama. Leaving part of his force to hold Chagres, he began the long and gruelling march across the Isthmus to the richest city of the Spanish Main.

At last they stood on the open savanna before the city of Panama, with the Spanish cavalry galloping towards them. Suddenly, the grand and disciplined charge dissolved into chaos. The cavalry had ridden into swampy ground, and the weight of horse and man sank them to the animals knees at every step. Morgan seized his chance and his men poured withering volleys at the floundering horsemen, virtually wiping them out. The buccaneers advanced towards the infantry.

At this point the Spaniards drove the wild bulls forward. But the buccaneers stood their ground and fired into the charging cattle, and the volley of musketry so frightened the bulls that they scattered in all directions, a large body turning back and stampeding into the Spanish infantry. The buccaneers advanced with a victory yell and after a further battle completely defeated the Spanish army and took the city.

The sacking of Panama is one of the great atrocities of history. Morgan's horde of ravenous scoundrels behaved like wild beasts. They killed, tortured, and plundered on a vast scale. Then, after the orgy of bloodshed, the looted city was set alight and Panama razed to the ground. The drunken buccaneers staggered from the blazing city loaded down with booty but most of them were not to enjoy their stolen wealth.

For Morgan, the master schemer, had formed a plan to cheat his men out of their share of the plunder. When they returned to Chagres the victorious buccaneers once again indulged in a drunken debauch.

They awoke to find that Morgan and a group of his closest confederates had gone, taking all the ships and all the treasure. But Morgan, too was in for a surprise.

When he returned to Jamaica he found that Modyford had been replaced by a new governor, one who made it clear he was not going to tolerate piracy or support privateering. Morgan was summoned to England by the King to answer for his violation of the treaty with Spain, and the charges of piracy laid against him.

But 'Morgan's Luck' held good. In England the public treated him as a hero – in the style of Drake – a highly successful hero who had taught the Spaniards a lesson. Then the political situation with Spain took a different turn, and instead of being punished, Morgan was made a knight and sent back to Jamaica as Lieutenant Governor, with the duty to 'suppress the trade of buccaneering'!

Morgan served his King well in his new office, and dealt harshly with buccaneers brought before him. And although he suffered a brief fall from favour in 1682, when Sir Henry Morgan, ex-buccaneer, died in 1688, he was a man of great wealth, power, and distinction.

The prophecy that came true
Josephine, Empress of France

One October day in Paris, in 1795, a fourteen-year-old boy presented himself before a young general. He had come on a mission of honour: to reclaim his father's sword. The sword had been confiscated, along with all other weapons in the area, a few days before. The boy explained that his father, now dead, had also been a general, and that it was only fitting that the sword should be returned. The officer, moved by the request and the dignity of the boy, gave him the sword. The lad's name was Eugène Beauharnais; the twenty-six-year-old general was Napoleon Bonaparte.

Eugène's mother, the widowed Madame de Beauharnais, was extremely grateful to General Bonaparte, whom she had heard about but never met, and she called on him the next day to thank him for his generosity. The visit was to be the beginning of one of history's most famous romances. The general would become an Emperor, and Madame de Beauharnais would reign as the Empress Josephine.

Their life together would fulfil a prophecy given to the young widow many years before, in her childhood on the West Indian island of Martinique. An old native woman, called Euphemia, had told the girl that she would soon be married; that after much unhappiness she would become a widow; but that one day she would be crowned Queen of France.

The prophecy struck the girl, and her family, as ridiculous. What possible chance was there for a girl from an impoverished, though well-connected colonial family to become Queen of France She was, without doubt, a pretty young girl, with beautiful blue eyes and a remarkably gentle and musical voice, but these qualities hardly seemed to qualify her for the role of Queen of France.

Josephine Tascher – or, to give her the full name with which she was christened, Marie-Josephe-Rose de Tascher de la Pagerie – was born on 23 June 1763. Her grandfather, a member of an old family of French gentry, had sailed to Martinique in 1726. Neither he nor his son Joseph-Gaspard, Josephine's father, had prospered. Joseph-Gaspard was an obscure sugar-planter, and although he was fortunate enough to marry into one of the oldest and most respected families on the island, his life was plagued by ill health, and his business affairs were seldom far from bankruptcy.

He was delighted, therefore, when the Marquis de Beauharnais, who had been governor of Martinique at the time of Josephine's birth, suggested a marriage between his son Alexander, who was a young army officer, and Josephine. Alexander and his father were now living in Paris, and after the terms of the marriage had been agreed, Josephine and her father began the long voyage to France.

In October 1779 they sailed into the harbour at Brest, where Alexander was waiting anxiously to see his bride-to-be, whom he had last seen when he was six years old and she a baby.

Eight weeks later the young couple were married, and they settled down in Paris, in the luxurious home of the Marquis, Alexander's father.

The marriage got off to a bad start. Her soldier husband almost immediately went away to serve with his regiment, throwing his sixteen-year-old bride back on her own resources. Josephine rapidly developed a taste for extravagant living, and, even more unfortunate for the marriage, she began going out with other men. Over the next ten years, although she bore Alexander two children, the boy Eugène and a girl, Hortense, the couple grew further and further apart. Alexander devoted his energies to his career and Josephine devoted hers to climbing rung after rung of the social ladder. Expensive clothes, glittering parties, splendid banquets; this became her world, and it turned her head completely.

It was a world soon to be brutally shattered by the upheavals of the French Revolution. But few in high society foresaw what was to come. To them the world, their world, looked secure and permanent.

In 1788, with her two children, Josephine made the long journey back to the land of her birth. She left France on the eve of one of the greatest revolutions in history, and she returned into its midst.

When she arrived back in Paris in the feverish atmosphere of late 1790 she found that Alexander was a prominent member of the Revolutionary Party. The two became reconciled and Josephine was immediately back in the limelight, only this time basking in the reflected glory of her husband. Although she herself had no interest in politics, except as they affected her personally, she was swept along by her husband's meteoric rise to power. In 1791 he became, for a period president of the Constituent Assembly, the effective government of France, and the body charged with rewriting the constitution. Josephine was no longer Madame de Beauharnais. She was *citoyenne* ('citizenness') Beauharnais – equality was the popular cry. It was the climax of Alexander's political career. And it brought him one step nearer death.

For Alexander was not a revolutionary. He was a liberal aristocrat, passionately desiring fundamental changes in French government and French life. But he recoiled in horror from the prospect of turning the streets of Paris red with blood. As so often happens in a revolution, people of moderate views, who set the wheels of reform in motion, become the eventual victims of the violent upheaval they have unwittingly triggered off.

Over the next three years, as the power shifted from men like Beauharnais to implacable revolutionaries like Danton and Robespierre, heads began to roll. The Paris mob clamoured for blood, aristocratic blood. Beauharnais returned to his duties in the army, and then retired to the country, where he hoped to avoid attention. But it was to no avail. Even the executions in 1793 of King Louis XVI and his Queen, Marie Antoinette, were not enough. The eyes of the Jacobins, an extremist group led by Robespierre, increasingly turned on their old comrades-in-arms. Having guillotined a king and a queen, eliminating former colleagues could be regarded as fairly routine. The Terror was on.

One by one the old friends of the Revolution perished under the pitiless knife. In March 1794 Alexander was arrested. The next month Josephine was sent to prison. In June, Alexander went bravely to his death on the scaffold, ironically only three days before the Revolutionary Tribunal, now in fear for its life, summoned up the courage to overthrow the dreaded Robespierre. The 'architect of the Terror' swiftly followed his many victims to the guillotine. With his death the bloody executions ground to a halt; just in time to save Josephine, who would certainly have shared her husband's fate.

She was released and once more reunited with her children. The Revolution went forward, but its most turbulent phase was over. Josephine began to pick up the pieces of her shattered life. With Eugène and Hortense she moved into a house on Rue Chantereine, a house that would become famous as the home of the newly-wed Napoleon Bonaparte.

Napoleon fell in love with Josephine almost at first sight. Over the next few hectic months, while he was making preparations to assume command of the Army of Italy, he courted her ardently, and on 8 March 1796 they were married. The impoverished young Corsican brought almost nothing to the marriage except love and ambition. But his prospects were glittering.

Their marriage began on a comical note. On the wedding night Josephine's pet dog Fortuné, was not at all pleased at being ordered out of bed, his accustomed sleeping place. Having scant respect for rank, he bit the great general on the leg.

Only three days later Napoleon set off for Italy. Over the next year Josephine was to have only fleeting glimpses of her new husband, for he was fighting the campaign in Italy that was to make him a household name throughout France. One after another the spectacular victories were won by the great conqueror: Arcole, Rivoli, Castiglione, names of obscure Italian villages that would go down in French history as the opening pages of the great Bonaparte legend.

When he returned to Paris it was to a hero's

welcome. The name Bonaparte was on everyone's lips. People cheered him when he appeared on the streets. But his return was marred by the discovery that Josephine had been unfaithful to him.

Bored by the gay life of Paris and furious with his wife, Napoleon was soon off again; this time to Egypt where he hoped, by a secret invasion, to cripple England's Mediterranean sea power. In his absence Josephine purchased the beautiful estate of Malmaison, near Paris. She threw herself into the task of converting it to almost regal splendour. Exquisite furniture filled the rooms; priceless works of art adorned the walls. She lavished a fortune on her new surroundings, so that when her husband returned, in the autumn of 1799, it was to a home worthy of a conqueror. Napoleon was not particularly impressed. All he could see about him was luxury and idleness, and he had important work to do.

He at once plunged into the fray of political life. France was in perilous straits, at war with almost every other country in Europe. The survival of Revolutionary France was at stake. It was the hour for a great leader to rise. Napoleon was ready. Almost immediately, the government was overthrown, and with one bloodless stroke Bonaparte became master of France, First Consul for life.

Their new official residence was the Luxembourg, the beautiful palace in the Tuileries. The Luxembourg began, once again, to take on the trappings of a royal court. Josephine was well suited to the role of First Lady. She began to take her husband more seriously, at last shaking herself free from her past. Now on the very centre of the world stage she played her part with grace and dignity. The childhood in the tropics, and the dangerous hectic years of the Revolu-

A bust of Napoleon Bonaparte
when he was First Consul.

tion were only a distant memory.

She had only four years to wait before becoming
Queen of France. On 2 December, 1804, at the altar
of Notre Dame Cathedral, Napoleon, immediately
after crowning himself Emperor, placed a crown upon
his wife's head and declared her Empress of France.
The old Martinique prediction of her childhood had
come true. Fortune had carried Josephine to the very
pinnacle of world fame. And her husband was the
most powerful single man in the world.

But still it was war, and more war. Year after year
the stunning victories of Napoleon Bonaparte rocked
the world. Yet as his triumphs mounted up, he found
he had another cause for concern. He had built an
empire. He could fight to defend it. But who would
succeed him? Into whose hands could he pass it? Josephine had failed to provide him with an heir. Would

his life's work pass to a stranger, or even worse, would it collapse altogether upon his death?

This lack of an heir became an obsession with him. Nothing was more important than the continuance of the Empire. Any sacrifice must be made. Inevitably the sacrifice had to be Josephine. On 30 November 1809, after a meal eaten in almost complete silence, the servants were dismissed. Napoleon bluntly informed Josephine that in the interest of the nation their marriage must be brought to an end. Josephine could do nothing but accept the decision.

The marriage was annulled. Josephine retired to Malmaison, well provided for, but alone. Her part on the world stage was finished.

Yet Napoleon's role too, was about to come to an end. Although he took a new bride almost immediately, Princess Marie Louise of Austria, and was duly presented with an heir, his dreams of everlasting empire were soon to be shattered. Crushing defeats in 1812, in Russia, and Spain and Portugal, turned the tide against the once-invincible Bonaparte. The next two years were utterly disastrous. One by one his allies turned against him. The combined might of Europe moved in for the kill. The armies of France, reeling before the onslaught, fell back on Paris. The Empire crumbled. On 30 March 1814 Paris fell, and three days later Napoleon was deposed.

It was nearly the end for Bonaparte. For Josephine it was the end. Her life began to ebb away, as she watched Bonaparte's utter collapse from her Malmaison retreat. Less than two months later, on 29 May, she died, just short of her fifty-first birthday. But the Napoleon who sorrowfully received the news was no longer the strong man of Europe. He was an exile on the Mediterranean island of Elba.

'Here comes Calamity'

Calamity Jane, the wildest woman in the West

Deadwood City, South Dakota, was a wild frontier town of the American West in the 1870's. Gold had been found in the Black Hills and hundreds of tough miners flocked to the town, followed by the usual crowd of gamblers, desperadoes, saloon keepers, and dance-hall girls.

In this whisky-sodden atmosphere of gold fever, greed, gunfights, and reckless spending, it is not surprising that Deadwood was inhabited by a legion of untamed, hell-raising characters. And one of the wildest was a woman – Calamity Jane.

Her legend is a compound of fact and fiction, of high adventure and low living. Many of her supposed exploits are the product of imaginative writers and film makers, but much of her real life is well documented. People who knew her have left vivid accounts of her boisterous actions and adventures.

Calamity Jane, it seems, was a miscast by nature. For she dressed, drank, cursed, smoked, and chewed tobacco like a man. She was neither beautiful nor ugly; her plain face was square-jawed and sun-bronzed. But her face and shapely figure were made less attractive by her habit of wearing a battered old hat and buckskin suit. In this rig she looked like, and lived the life of, a hardy frontiersman.

The gun-slinging Calamity Jane, in her battered old hat and buckskin coat. As tough as any frontiersman, she was as skilled with a gun as she was rough with her tongue. Below–Calamity Jane as a little girl, in the uniform of a cavalry officer. Even as a youngster she preferred to wear boy's clothes.

Her exact birthdate and birthplace are not known, but it is generally believed she was born in Missouri in 1848. Her real name was Martha Jane Canarray. As a youngster she lived with her family on a farm near Marion Township. Even then she preferred wearing boy's clothes rather than the fussy, hampering dress of a girl.

She travelled west with the family in 1863. Not much is known about her activities during the next few years. She is said to have married and lived for a while in Virginia City. Then came her years of roaming through the West, drifting from town to town, working in a variety of jobs, and becoming a familiar figure on the frontier.

She had handled firearms since she was a child on the farm, but during her years of wandering she developed skill with pistol and rifle until she was the equal of most of the noted gunmen who populated the trigger happy West. An old pioneer once claimed that 'she gave the finest demonstration of firearms' he had ever seen. She was also an expert rider and could handle with case a team of horses or mules.

Martha Jane could hold her own against any man, and she was not afraid of man's work. She had an arduous job as a labourer on the Union Pacific Railroad, and at times was employed as a mule skinner (mule driver), a job noted for its hard work and long hours. By 1870 Martha Jane's reputation as a lusty, whisky-swilling character, with an explosive temper and ready gun, was well-established. She was notorious for her wildness in such towns as Cheyenne, Abilene, and Hays City, and no man in his right mind dared take liberties with her.

It was about this time that she came to Deadwood. And it was here that she gained her famous nickname, 'Calamity Jane'. It was her custom when she had taken too much to drink to 'hurrah' the town, or kick up a din. She would swagger into a crowded saloon, push her way to the bar, bang her fist down for whisky, and the other customers would grin knowingly and call out: 'Here comes Calamity.' In other words, here comes trouble.

And she lived up to her name. Often she would fire off her revolvers in the saloon, breaking mirrors and bottles and making the customers dive for cover. She would roll along the street singing at the top of her voice and howling like a wolf.

There is another version of the origin of her nickname. It is that while she was serving as a scout with the U.S. Cavalry in 1872, she galloped forward into the midst of hostile Indians and dramatically rescued a wounded officer, thus saving him from a 'calamity' at the hands of the warriors, who often tortured their captives before killing them. But most historians of the Wild West view this claim with scepticism and much prefer the Deadwood 'saloon-busting' version.

Jane is also known to have driven the famous Deadwood Stage, which travelled between Deadwood and Cheyenne, and to have served as shotgun guard. The mail coach was often attacked by bandits, and on one occasion, when the driver was killed, Jane grabbed the reins, and lashing the horses into a frenzied gallop, drove the coach safely to its destination. Another time when a mountain lion sprang on to the back of one of the horses, Jane instantly killed the wild beast with a single shot from the violently swaying coach.

Calamity Jane saves the Deadwood Stage from the fury of a mountain lion. As driver and shotgun guard on this famous Stage she had ample scope to prove her accuracy with a gun.

It was in Deadwood that her legend bloomed to its fullness. And it was here that the colourful, deadly 'Wild Bill' Hickok rode into her life. Hickok was a flamboyant figure, a fancy dresser, almost a dandy. He was a tall, slim man with long fair hair to his shoulders and a luxurious cavalry-styled moustache. He had a high reputation as a gunfighter and had killed a number of men.

Hickok had served as a police officer in several towns but he was not a dedicated lawman. He would rather gamble with the criminal element than bother himself to put them behind bars. And, when put to the test, he would rather kill a man than bring him to justice by trial. His wide reputation as the 'Prince of Pistoleers' had been built up by writers from the East who penned extravagant stories about him for magazines and cheap novels. He also appeared in a road show called 'Scouts of the Prairie' with Buffalo Bill Cody. Nevertheless, Hickok was acknowledged as a marksman of note and a dangerous man to tangle with.

Calamity Jane was immediately attracted to Hickok, greatly admiring him, and a friendship developed that she treasured all her life. Exactly what kind of relationship it was is not clear. Some writers have suggested there was real romance between the two. It is also claimed that Calamity and Wild Bill were actually married for a short while, and that he left her because he was shocked and ashamed of her crude and vulgar behaviour. Jane herself, later in life, denied that they had ever been more than good friends.

But there is no doubt whatever that she thought a great deal of him. And she never really got over his sudden death in Deadwood in 1876.

Hickok was murdered in cowardly fashion by Jack McCall, a nobody who stole a place in Western history by this one and only noteworthy act. At the time Wild Bill was playing draw poker in the Carl Mann saloon. He was sitting with his back towards the door, an unusual position for him as he had long adopted the habit of sitting with his back towards the wall, so that his enemies – and he had many – could not attack him from the rear.

But on this occasion he was late at the table and his

favourite chair had been taken. He asked one of the players to change places with him but the man declined. Rather than make a fuss, Hickok shrugged his shoulders and sat down in the empty chair. When the card game was well in progress, Jack McCall entered the saloon and gradually sidled up behind Wild Bill. He then quickly drew a revolver and, at a distance of three feet, fired a bullet into the back of Hickok's head.

Such were Hickok's lightning reflexes that as the bullet hit him he half rose from the chair and clutched at the butts of his pistols, partially drawing the right-hand gun. Then he crashed forward across the table, dead. He had been holding five cards: two aces, two eights, and a queen, a draw poker hand known ever afterwards as 'The Dead Man's Hand'.

Legend has it that, after the shooting, when McCall ran out of the saloon and, in a state of panic, hid in a butcher's shop, Calamity Jane went after him and chased him around the shop with a meat cleaver. But if this incident had been true Jack McCall would never have survived Jane's angry vengeance. As it was, McCall eventually suffered for his cold-blooded deed on the gallows. At his trial he paid high tribute to Hickok. When asked: 'Why didn't you go around in front of Wild Bill and shoot him in the face like a man ' McCall answered honestly, 'I didn't want to commit suicide.'

Hickok was buried at Deadwood. Grief-stricken at his death Jane left the town and drifted aimlessly like the tumbleweed. She drank more heavily, and related fanciful stories about her exploits with, and her admiration for, Wild Bill. She caught the ear of a writer and became the 'heroine' of a cheap novel called *White Devil of Yellowstone*. And so her legend grew.

Always in need of money she agreed to appear on the stage and was billed as:

'Calamity Jane! The famous woman scout
of the Wild West! Heroine of a thousand
thrilling adventures! The terror of evil-doers
in the Black Hills! The comrade of
Buffalo Bill and Wild Bill! See this famous
woman and hear her graphic descriptions
of her daring exploits!'

She toured Chicago, St. Louis, and Kansas City with the show. But because of her drinking and erratic behaviour she was soon fired.

Although Jane demanded respectful attention while she herself was on stage, she did not extend such courtesy to others. On one of her frequent visits to Deadwood, for instance, a bandit named Arkansas Tom took her to see a play at the town's theatre. She did not like the performance of the leading lady and, at a highly dramatic moment of the play, Jane – who was chewing tobacco – stood up and let fly a stream of tobacco juice at the unfortunate actress, which ruined her beautiful pink dress. Pandemonium broke out, pierced by the screams of the enraged actress. Jane calmly flung a gold coin on the stage and said, 'That's for your damn silly dress', and walked out of the house, arm in arm with the smiling bandit.

In spite of Jane's wild ways the people of Deadwood regarded her with amused tolerance, even respect. She had courage, and a real tenderness, under her tough exterior. When Deadwood was swept by a smallpox epidemic she risked her life daily by helping the town's only physician, and caring for the sick and dying, especially the children. Many survived the epidemic because of her rough but efficient nursing.

When the emergency was over Jane left Deadwood again. As the years went by she continued to roam the Western frontier, leaving a trail of minor calamity behind her. In one town she wrecked a saloon and blacked the eyes of two peace officers. And so it went on.

In July 1903 she turned up at the Galloway Hotel in Terry, not far from Deadwood. She was desperately ill. The years of dissolute living had taken their toll. She was fifty-five years old but looked seventy. Her hair was grey, and her once smooth, sun-bronzed face was now like a shrivelled lemon.

Several weeks later she was dying. She opened her eyes and whispered, 'What's the date?' When told it was 2 August she replied, 'It's the twenty-seventh anniversary of Bill's death . . . bury me next to Wild Bill'. Those were her last words. She died shortly after.

Her funeral was the largest that Deadwood had ever seen. The people respected her dying wish and she was buried at the Mount Moriah Cemetery alongside the man she had admired so much. And there they lie today, two Western drifters who finally came to rest on the shore of legend.